14 DAYS PRAYER TO BREAK EVIL PATTERNS

TIMOTHY ATUNNISE

GLOVIM PUBLISHING HOUSE
ATLANTA, GEORGIA

BREAKING EVIL PATTERNS

Copyright © 2023 by Timothy Atunnise

All rights reserved. No part of this book may be reproduced, copied, stored or transmitted in any form or by any means – graphic, electronic, or mechanical, including photocopying, recording, or information storage and retrieval systems without the prior written permission of Glovim Publishing House except where permitted by law.

Unless otherwise specified, all Scripture quotations in this book are from The Holy Bible, King James Version. KJV is Public domain in the United States printed in 1987.

Glovim Publishing House
1078 Citizens Pkwy
Suite A
Morrow, Georgia 30260

glovimbooks@gmail.com
www.glovimonline.org

Printed in the United States of America

IMPORTANT NOTICE

Deliverance is a benefit of the Kingdom, only for the children of God. If you have not accepted Jesus Christ as your personal Lord and Savior, this is the best time to do so.

Before you continue, if you want to exercise authority and power in the name of Jesus Christ, you need to be sure you are in right standing with God. The Bible says,
"Then he called his twelve disciples together, and gave them power and authority over all devils, and to cure diseases." - Luke 9:1

"And these signs shall follow them that believe; in my name shall they cast out devils; they shall speak with new tongues; they shall take up serpents; and if they drink any deadly thing, it shall not hurt them; they shall lay hands on the sick, and they shall recover." – Mark 16:17-18.

These are promises for the Children of God, not just for everyone. Why don't you give your life to Christ today and you will have access to the same promises. Food that is meant for the children will not be given to dogs.

"But he answered and said, it is not meet to take the children's bread, and cast it to dogs" – Matthew 15:26.

If you really want to be delivered from any bondage of the wicked and be set free from any form of captivity, I ask you today to give your life to Christ. If you are ready, say this prayer with all your heart:

"Dear Heavenly Father, You have called me to Yourself in the name of Your dear Son Jesus Christ. I realize that Jesus Christ is the only Way, the Truth, and the Life.

I acknowledge to You that I am a sinner. I believe that Your only begotten Son Jesus Christ shed His precious blood on the cross, died for my sins, and rose again on the third day. I am truly sorry for the deeds which I have committed against You, and therefore, I am willing to repent (turn away from my sins). Have mercy on me, a sinner. Cleanse me and forgive me of my sins.

I truly desire to serve You, Lord Jesus. Starting from now, I pray that You would help me to hear Your still small voice. Lord, I desire to be led by Your Holy Spirit so I can faithfully follow You and obey all of Your commandments. I ask You for the strength to love You more than anything else, so I won't fall back into my old ways. I also ask You to bring genuine believers into my life who will encourage me to live for You and help me stay accountable.

Jesus, I am truly grateful for Your grace which has led me to repentance and has saved me from my sins. By the indwelling of Your Holy Spirit, I now have the power to overcome all sin which before so easily entangled me. Lord Jesus, please transform my life so that I may bring glory and honor to You alone and not to myself.

Right now, I confess Jesus Christ as the Lord of my life. With my heart, I believe that God the Father raised His Son Jesus Christ from the dead. This very moment I acknowledge that Jesus Christ is my Savior and according to His Word, right now I am born again. Thank You Jesus, for coming into my life and hearing my prayer. I ask all of this in the name of my Lord and Savior, Jesus Christ. Amen".

I hereby congratulate and welcome you into the Kingdom. You hereby have full access to the benefits, promises and blessings of the Kingdom.

This book is loaded with blessings, you will not be disappointed as you continue to enjoy the goodness of the Lord.

INSTRUCTIONS

If you are new to this method of prayer, please follow this instruction carefully:

Step 1:

Spend enough time in praising and worshiping God not just for what He is about to do or what He has done, but WHO HE IS.

Step 2:

Unforgiveness will surely hinder your prayer, take time to remember all those who have done you wrong, and forgive them from the bottom of your heart. THIS IS VERY IMPORTANT BECAUSE YOUR DELIVERANCE DEPENDS ON IT.

Step 3:

Believe in your heart that God will answer your prayer when you call upon Him, and do not doubt in your heart.

Step 4:

Pray in the name of Jesus Christ alone.

Step 5:

Repeat each prayer point 25 to 30 times or until you are convinced that you have received the answer before you go to the next prayer point. Example: When you take prayer point number 1, you say this prayer over and over again, 25 – 30 times or until you are convinced that you have an answer before you go to prayer point number 2.

Step 6:

It will be more effective if you can fast along with your prayer. If you want total deliverance from your bondage, take 3 days of sacrifice in fasting as you say your prayer aggressively, asking your situation to receive permanent solution and YOUR DELIVERANCE WILL BE MADE PERFECT IN THE NAME OF JESUS CHRIST. AMEN!

Table of Contents

Important Notice..4

Instructions 6

Day One...11

Day Two 21

Day Three 33

Day Four..43

Day Five 53

Day Six..63

Day Seven..73

Day Eight...81

Day Nine..89

Day Ten 99

Day Eleven 107

Day Twelve 117

Day Thirteen..125

Day Fourteen 135

"But this kind does not go out except by prayer and fasting."
- Matthew 17:21

DAY 1

Breaking Generational Patterns of Evil or Negative Influences

One of the remarkable aspects of our existence is the intergenerational flow of traits, behaviors, and even values within families. While this transmission can be a source of blessings and wisdom, it can also perpetuate negative influences and patterns of evil. However, as individuals of faith, we can rely on the transformative power of God's Word to break free from these destructive cycles. Today, we will explore how scripture provides guidance and encouragement for breaking generational patterns of evil and negative influences within our families.

- Recognizing the Influence of Generational Patterns:
  The first step toward breaking generational patterns is acknowledging their existence. We must be willing to examine our family history and honestly identify negative behaviors or influences that have been passed down. This self-reflection aligns with the teaching of Proverbs 28:13: "Whoever conceals their sins does not prosper, but the one who confesses and renounces them finds mercy." By acknowledging these patterns, we open ourselves to God's mercy and transformation.

- Seeking God's Forgiveness:
  Breaking generational patterns requires seeking God's forgiveness for our own actions and the sins of our ancestors. Ezekiel 18:31 says, "Rid yourselves of all the offenses you have committed and get a new heart and a new spirit." Through

repentance, we can find renewal in Christ and break free from the negative influences of the past. God's forgiveness gives us the strength to forge a new path for ourselves and future generations.

- Embracing Personal Responsibility:
  While it is crucial to recognize the impact of our family history, it is equally important to understand that we have the power to make different choices. Everyone has the ability to reject destructive behaviors and embrace a life aligned with God's truth. Galatians 5:1 reminds us, *"It is for freedom that Christ has set us free. Stand firm, then, and do not let yourselves be burdened again by a yoke of slavery."* By relying on God's strength, we can break free from the chains of generational patterns.

- Renewing the Mind with God's Word:
  The Bible serves as a powerful tool for transforming our minds and reshaping our behavior. Romans 12:2 urges us, *"Do not conform to the pattern of this world but be transformed by the renewing of your mind."* By immersing ourselves in God's Word, we can gain wisdom, insight, and discernment to break free from negative influences. His truth illuminates our path and empowers us to make righteous choices for ourselves and future generations.

- Building a Foundation on Godly Principles:
  To break generational patterns, we must establish a new foundation based on godly principles. Matthew 7:24-25 illustrates the importance of a solid foundation: *"Therefore, everyone who hears these words of mine and puts them into practice is like a wise man who built his house on the rock... It did not fall, because it had its foundation on the rock."* By

aligning our lives with God's principles, we establish a firm groundwork that can withstand the negative influences of the past.

Breaking generational patterns of evil or negative influences within our families is an empowering journey that requires self-reflection, repentance, personal responsibility, and a firm foundation in God's Word. Through His grace, we can break free from the chains of the past and create a new legacy for ourselves and future generations. As we walk in faith, let us remember the words of 2 Corinthians 5:17: *"Therefore, if anyone is in Christ, the new creation has come: The old has gone, the new is here!"*

Confession & Declaration:

In the name of Jesus, I declare that the powers of darkness operating against me are broken! According to Ephesians 6:12, *"For we do not wrestle against flesh and blood, but against the rulers, against the authorities, against the cosmic powers over this present darkness, against the spiritual forces of evil in the heavenly places."* I stand firm in the authority I have in Christ, and I rebuke every demonic force that seeks to hinder my progress and well-being.

I declare that I am a child of God, redeemed by the blood of Jesus. Romans 8:37 declares, *"No, in all these things we are more than conquerors through him who loved us."* I reject any power of darkness that tries to intimidate or oppress me, for I am more than a conqueror through Christ!

I declare that I am filled with the Holy Spirit and His power resides within me. 2 Timothy 1:7 assures me that *"God gave us a spirit not of fear but of power and love and self-control."* I reject fear and any stronghold of darkness, knowing that I have the power to overcome through the Spirit of God.

I declare that every curse spoken against me is nullified by the power of the cross. Galatians 3:13 says, *"Christ redeemed us from the curse of the law by becoming a curse for us."* I proclaim my freedom from every generational curse, every spoken curse, and every witchcraft attack. I am washed clean by the blood of Jesus.

I declare that I walk in the light of God's truth, and the lies of darkness have no power over me. Psalm 27:1 affirms, *"The Lord is my light and my salvation; whom shall I fear?"* I reject every lie, deception, and manipulation of the enemy. I stand on the truth of God's Word and declare victory over the powers of darkness.

I stand firm in these declarations, knowing that God's Word is powerful and cannot be broken, and that God is faithful to bring deliverance and victory in every area of my life. I trust in His promises and rest in His unfailing love.

Prayer of Deliverance

1. Heavenly Father, I come before you today, declaring that enough is enough in breaking generational patterns of evil in my family line. I renounce and reject every negative influence passed down through my ancestors.
2. Lord, I thank you for your mercy and grace that enables me to break free from the chains of generational bondage. I declare that the power of the cross of Jesus Christ breaks every curse and negative pattern over my life and my family.
3. I repent on behalf of my ancestors for any involvement in idolatry, witchcraft, occult practices, or any form of rebellion against you, O God. I ask for your forgiveness and cleansing.

4. I declare that I am a child of the Most High God, and I am no longer subject to the curses and negative influences of the past. I am redeemed by the blood of Jesus, and I walk in the freedom and authority that comes from being in Christ.
5. Heavenly Father, I break and renounce every curse of poverty that has plagued my family line. I decree that I am blessed to be a blessing, and I walk in the abundance and prosperity that you have ordained for me.
6. I cancel and nullify every negative pronouncement and evil decree that has been spoken over my life and my family. I declare that no weapon formed against me shall prosper, and every tongue that rises against me in judgment shall be condemned.
7. I reject the spirit of fear and anxiety that has been passed down through my family line. I command it to leave my life and my mind in the name of Jesus. I receive the spirit of power, love, and a sound mind.
8. I break every generational cycle of addiction and bondage in my family. I decree that I am free from every form of addiction, whether it be drugs, alcohol, pornography, or any other destructive behavior. I walk in the liberty and self-control that the Holy Spirit provides.
9. I renounce and break every generational pattern of sickness and disease that has plagued my family. I declare that by the stripes of Jesus, I am healed and made whole. I release the healing power of God to flow through every cell of my body.
10. Lord, I pray for the restoration of broken relationships within my family. I break every spirit of division, strife, and unforgiveness. I decree that love, peace, and reconciliation will prevail in my family.
11. I cancel and break every curse of marital failure and divorce in my family line. I decree that my marriage is blessed, strong,

and built on the foundation of your love and grace. I declare that my spouse and I will walk in unity and harmony.

12. I break and dismantle every generational pattern of sexual immorality and perversion in my family line. I decree that purity, faithfulness, and godly relationships will be the standard in my life and the lives of my future generations.
13. Lord, I break every curse of untimely death and premature endings in my family. I decree that I will live a long and fruitful life, fulfilling the purpose and destiny you have ordained for me.
14. I sever every ungodly soul tie and unhealthy emotional attachment that has been formed through my family line. I declare that I am free to love and receive love in a healthy and godly manner.
15. I renounce and break every curse of failure and lack that has plagued my family. I decree that I am destined for success and abundance in every area of my life. I am an overcomer through Christ Jesus.
16. Heavenly Father, I pray for the salvation and deliverance of every member of my family who has not yet come to know you. I decree that they will encounter your love and mercy, and their hearts will be transformed by the power of the Holy Spirit.
17. I cancel and nullify every negative word spoken over my life and my family. I declare that the words of my mouth and the meditation of my heart are pleasing to you, O God.
18. I renounce and break every curse of generational strife and division in my family. I decree that unity, love, and respect will reign supreme among us. We will walk in harmony and purpose.
19. I break and dismantle every generational pattern of mental illness and emotional instability in my family line. I declare that I have the mind of Christ, and my emotions are anchored in the peace and joy that comes from the Holy Spirit.

20. I reject and renounce every spirit of rejection and abandonment that has plagued my family line. I declare that I am accepted and beloved by God, and I walk in the fullness of his love and acceptance.
21. Lord, I break every curse of generational debt and financial bondage in my family line. I decree that I am a good steward of the resources you have entrusted to me, and I walk in financial freedom and abundance.
22. I renounce and break every curse of generational dishonesty and deceit in my family. I declare that I am a person of integrity and honesty, and I walk in the truth of your Word.
23. I break and sever every curse of generational laziness and lack of productivity in my family line. I decree that I am diligent, hardworking, and productive in all that I do. I am a vessel of honor and excellence.
24. Lord, I break every curse of generational unbelief and spiritual blindness in my family. I decree that my family and I will have eyes to see, ears to hear, and hearts to understand your truth. We will walk in faith and spiritual discernment.
25. I reject and break every curse of generational pride and arrogance in my family line. I humble myself before you, O God, and I walk in humility and teachability. I give all glory and honor to you.
26. I break and dismantle every generational pattern of violence and anger in my family. I decree that I am filled with the fruit of the Spirit, which is love, joy, peace, patience, kindness, goodness, faithfulness, gentleness, and self-control.
27. I renounce and break every curse of generational infertility and barrenness in my family line. I decree that I am blessed to be fruitful and multiply, and I release the blessing of children and a legacy of faith to future generations.
28. Lord, I break every curse of generational spiritual apathy and lukewarmness in my family. I decree that my family and I will

be passionate and on fire for you. We will serve you wholeheartedly and make a difference in the world.

29. I reject and break every curse of generational confusion and indecisiveness in my family line. I decree that I have the mind of Christ, and I make wise and discerning decisions by the leading of the Holy Spirit.
30. Heavenly Father, I break every curse of generational racism and prejudice in my family. I decree that I am a bridge builder and a peacemaker, embracing and celebrating the diversity of your creation.
31. I renounce and break every curse of generational fear of failure and missed opportunities in my family line. I decree that I am bold and courageous, stepping out in faith to fulfill the purpose and calling you have placed on my life.
32. I break and sever every curse of generational unfaithfulness and infidelity in my family. I decree that I am faithful and committed in my relationships, honoring the covenant of marriage and the bonds of friendship.
33. I reject and renounce every spirit of generational pride and self-righteousness in my family line. I declare that I am clothed in the righteousness of Christ, and my identity is found in him alone.
34. Lord, I break every curse of generational spiritual dryness and stagnation in my family. I decree that my family and I will continually be refreshed and filled with the fire of the Holy Spirit. We will hunger and thirst for your presence.
35. I renounce and break every curse of generational rebellion and disobedience in my family line. I decree that I am submitted to your authority, O God, and I walk in obedience to your Word.
36. I break and dismantle every pattern of generational untimely accidents, death, and tragedies in my family. I decree that my family and I are protected by the blood of Jesus, and we walk in divine safety and divine providence.

37. I reject and break every curse of generational sexual immorality and impurity in my family line. I decree that I am pure and holy, presenting my body as a living sacrifice, pleasing to you, O God.
38. Lord, I break every curse of generational spiritual blindness and deception in my family. I decree that the eyes of our understanding are enlightened, and we walk in the revelation and knowledge of your truth.
39. I renounce and break every curse of generational addiction to substances or behaviors in my family line. I decree that I am free from bondage, and I walk in the freedom and liberty that comes from being in Christ.
40. I break and dismantle every generational pattern of lack of purpose and direction in my family. I decree that I am divinely guided and empowered to fulfill the purpose and destiny you have ordained for me.
41. I reject and renounce every spirit of generational bitterness and unforgiveness in my family line. I decree that I am filled with forgiveness and grace, releasing every offense, and embracing reconciliation and restoration.
42. Lord, I break every curse of generational pride and self-sufficiency in my family. I decree that I am dependent on you, O God, and I walk in humility and reliance on your strength and provision.
43. I renounce and break every curse of generational emotional wounds and traumas in my family line. I decree that I am healed and made whole by the power of your love and restoration.
44. I break and sever every curse of generational spiritual warfare and oppression in my family. I decree that I am more than a conqueror through Christ Jesus, and no weapon formed against me shall prosper.
45. I reject and break every curse of generational negative words and curses spoken over my life and my family. I decree that my

words are aligned with your truth, and I speak life, blessing, and encouragement over myself and others.
46. Lord, I break every curse of generational patterns of unbelief and doubt in my family line. I decree that I am rooted and grounded in faith, and I trust in your promises and the faithfulness of your Word.
47. I renounce and break every curse of generational pride and self-dependence in my family line. I decree that I am humble and reliant on your wisdom and guidance, O God.
48. I break and dismantle every generational pattern of financial struggles and lack in my family. I decree that I am blessed and prosperous in all that I do, and I am a channel of financial blessing to others.
49. I reject and renounce every spirit of generational fear and timidity in my family line. I decree that I am bold and courageous, walking in the authority and power that you have given me.
50. Lord, I break every curse of generational patterns of brokenness and dysfunction in my family. I decree that I am healed and restored, and I walk in wholeness and healthy relationships.
51. I renounce and break every curse of generational pride and self-centeredness in my family line. I decree that I am humble and compassionate, putting the needs of others before my own.
52. I break and sever every curse of generational patterns of violence and anger in my family line. I decree that I am filled with love, peace, and self-control, and I am an agent of reconciliation and peace.
53. Lord, I break every curse of generational patterns of spiritual blindness and deception in my family line. I decree that the truth of your Word shines brightly in our lives, and we walk in spiritual discernment and wisdom.

DAY 2

Deliverance from Spiritual Bondage: Seeking Liberation from Captivity

In the journey of life, we may encounter various challenges that go beyond the physical realm. Spiritual bondage is a condition where individuals find themselves trapped and enslaved by unseen forces, perpetuating evil patterns in their lives. However, there is hope for liberation through seeking the power and grace of God. Today, we will explore the concept of deliverance from spiritual bondage and discover how Scripture provides guidance and encouragement in breaking free from these strongholds.

- Recognizing Spiritual Bondage:
  The first step towards deliverance is acknowledging the presence of spiritual bondage in our lives. It could manifest in different ways, such as addictions, uncontrollable habits, fear, anger, or persistent negative patterns. The Bible affirms that our struggle is not against flesh and blood but against spiritual forces of evil (Ephesians 6:12). Awareness of this reality enables us to seek the freedom we desperately need.

- Repentance and Confession:
  True liberation begins with genuine repentance and confession of our sins before God. Psalm 32:5 says, *"Then I acknowledged my sin to you and did not cover up my iniquity. I said, 'I will confess my transgressions to the LORD.'"* As we humbly confess our sins and seek God's forgiveness, He cleanses us from all unrighteousness (1 John 1:9).

- Seeking God's Word:
  The Word of God is a powerful tool in breaking spiritual bondage. Jesus Himself declared, *"If you hold to my teaching, you are really my disciples. Then you will know the truth, and the truth will set you free"* (John 8:31-32). By immersing ourselves in Scripture, we gain wisdom, strength, and discernment to combat the lies and deception of the enemy.

- Prayer and Fasting:
  Prayer and fasting are essential disciplines in seeking deliverance from spiritual strongholds. Through fervent prayer, we connect with God, sharing our burdens and seeking His intervention. Jesus taught that some spiritual strongholds require both prayer and fasting for effective breakthrough (Matthew 17:21). Fasting helps us focus our hearts and minds on God, seeking His guidance and power to overcome the bondage we face.

- Submitting to God and Resisting the Enemy:
  James 4:7 provides a powerful formula for breaking free from spiritual bondage: *"Submit yourselves, then, to God. Resist the devil, and he will flee from you."* Surrendering our lives to God and submitting to His will opens the door for His divine intervention. As we resist the enemy's lies, temptations, and influences through the authority of Christ, we will experience the liberation He promises.

- Walking in Freedom:
  Once delivered from spiritual bondage, it is crucial to maintain a lifestyle of obedience and faithfulness. Galatians 5:1 reminds us, *"It is for freedom that Christ has set us free. Stand firm, then, and do not let yourselves be burdened again by a yoke of*

slavery." Embracing our freedom in Christ, we should continually renew our minds, guard our hearts, and surround ourselves with a supportive Christian community.

Deliverance from spiritual bondage is possible through the power of God. By recognizing our captivity, repenting of our sins, seeking God's Word, engaging in prayer and fasting, and submitting to God while resisting the enemy, we can experience true liberation. As we walk in freedom, let us remember Romans 8:37, which assures us that "in all these things we are more than conquerors through him who loved us." Trust in the Lord, for He is faithful to set you free and break the

Confession & Declaration:

In the name of Jesus, I declare that the powers of darkness operating against me are broken! According to Ephesians 6:12, *"For we do not wrestle against flesh and blood, but against the rulers, against the authorities, against the cosmic powers over this present darkness, against the spiritual forces of evil in the heavenly places."* I stand firm in the authority I have in Christ, and I rebuke every demonic force that seeks to hinder my progress and well-being.

I declare that I am a child of God, redeemed by the blood of Jesus. Romans 8:37 declares, *"No, in all these things we are more than conquerors through him who loved us."* I reject any power of darkness that tries to intimidate or oppress me, for I am more than a conqueror through Christ!

I declare that I am filled with the Holy Spirit and His power resides within me. 2 Timothy 1:7 assures me that *"God gave us a spirit not of fear but of power and love and self-control."* I reject fear and any stronghold of darkness, knowing that I have the power to overcome through the Spirit of God.

I declare that every curse spoken against me is nullified by the power of the cross. Galatians 3:13 says, *"Christ redeemed us from the curse of the law by becoming a curse for us."* I proclaim my freedom from every generational curse, every spoken curse, and every witchcraft attack. I am washed clean by the blood of Jesus.

I declare that I walk in the light of God's truth, and the lies of darkness have no power over me. Psalm 27:1 affirms, *"The Lord is my light and my salvation; whom shall I fear?"* I reject every lie, deception, and manipulation of the enemy. I stand on the truth of God's Word and declare victory over the powers of darkness.

I stand firm in these declarations, knowing that God's Word is powerful and cannot be broken, and that God is faithful to bring deliverance and victory in every area of my life. I trust in His promises and rest in His unfailing love.

Prayer of Deliverance

1. Heavenly Father, I come before you today, seeking deliverance from any spiritual bondage that has held me captive. Break every chain and stronghold in my life, in the name of Jesus Christ.
2. Lord, I repent for any sins or disobedience that have given the enemy legal rights to oppress and bind me. I renounce any involvement in occult practices or unholy alliances, and I ask for your forgiveness and cleansing, in the name of Jesus Christ.
3. I declare that Jesus Christ is Lord over my life, and I submit every area of my being to His authority. I renounce any false gods or idols that I have unknowingly served, and I surrender them to the power of the cross, in the name of Jesus Christ.

4. Holy Spirit, reveal to me any hidden sins or generational curses that have kept me bound. Shine your light into the darkest corners of my heart and bring them into alignment with your truth and freedom, in the name of Jesus Christ.
5. I break and cancel every evil covenant or pact that has been made on my behalf or by my ancestors. I declare that I am covered by the blood of Jesus, and no weapon formed against me shall prosper, in the name of Jesus Christ.
6. Heavenly Father, I plead the blood of Jesus over my mind, emotions, and will. I reject any tormenting thoughts or negative patterns that have plagued my thinking. I command every spirit of fear, anxiety, depression, and confusion to leave me now, in the name of Jesus Christ.
7. Lord, release your fire to consume every demonic influence that has hindered my spiritual growth and intimacy with you. Let your purifying flame burn away every impurity and stronghold in my life, in the name of Jesus Christ.
8. I declare that I am a child of God, and I have been bought with a price. I renounce any claim that the enemy has over my life, and I break free from his grip. I am no longer a slave but a beloved son/daughter of the Most High God, in the name of Jesus Christ.
9. Heavenly Father, I command every demonic assignment and plot against my life to be exposed and destroyed. Let the plans of the enemy be turned against him and let confusion reign in the camp of the adversary, in the name of Jesus Christ.
10. I speak to every demonic spirit that has been assigned to hinder my progress and destiny. I bind you in the name of Jesus and render you powerless. I command you to leave my life and never return, in the name of Jesus Christ.
11. Lord, I ask for a fresh anointing of your Holy Spirit to fill me and empower me to walk in victory. Let your anointing break

every yoke of bondage and set me free from every entanglement of the enemy, in the name of Jesus Christ.

12. I declare that I am more than a conqueror through Christ Jesus. No weapon formed against me shall prosper, and every tongue that rises against me in judgment shall be condemned, in the name of Jesus Christ.
13. I renounce and break any soul ties or ungodly connections that have kept me bound to toxic relationships or unhealthy patterns. I sever every unholy bond and declare freedom and restoration in my relationships, in the name of Jesus Christ.
14. Heavenly Father, I surrender my desires, ambitions, and dreams to your perfect will. I trust that you have a good plan for my life, and I ask for the grace to walk in obedience and surrender to your guidance, in the name of Jesus Christ.
15. I declare that I am delivered from every spirit of addiction or bondage. I am free from the chains of addiction to substances, behaviors, or unhealthy habits. The power of the Holy Spirit strengthens me to overcome every temptation, in the name of Jesus Christ.
16. Lord, I command every generational curse or hereditary bondage to be broken off my life. I declare that I am a new creation in Christ, and I am no longer subject to the sins of my ancestors. I walk in the freedom and righteousness of Jesus.
17. I speak to every spirit of poverty, lack, and financial bondage, and I command you to leave my life now. I declare that I am blessed and prosperous in every area, and I walk in the abundance that God has prepared for me, in the name of Jesus Christ.
18. Heavenly Father, I ask for the gift of discernment to recognize the schemes and tactics of the enemy. Open my eyes to see the spiritual battles around me and grant me the wisdom to stand firm in your truth, in the name of Jesus Christ.

19. I declare that every plan and assignment of the enemy to steal, kill, and destroy in my life is nullified and rendered powerless. I am hidden in the secret place of the Most High, and no evil shall befall me, in the name of Jesus Christ.
20. Lord, I break every curse of sickness and infirmity that has plagued my body. I release the healing power of Jesus Christ to flow through me, restoring health, vitality, and wholeness to every cell and organ, in the name of Jesus Christ.
21. I reject and renounce every lie and deception that the enemy has planted in my mind. I embrace the truth of God's Word, and I declare that I am a child of light, walking in the knowledge and revelation of Christ.
22. Heavenly Father, I ask for divine protection over my life and my loved ones. I plead the blood of Jesus over us, and I command every plan of the enemy to harm or destroy us to be thwarted and nullified, in the name of Jesus Christ.
23. I release forgiveness to those who have hurt or wronged me, knowing that unforgiveness can be a doorway for the enemy. I choose to let go of bitterness and resentment, and I ask for your grace to love and bless my enemies, in the name of Jesus Christ.
24. Lord, I surrender my dreams and ambitions to you. Align them with your perfect will and use them for your glory. I resist the temptation to pursue selfish desires and ask for a heart that is surrendered and obedient to you, in the name of Jesus Christ.
25. I declare that I am an overcomer by the blood of the Lamb and the word of my testimony. I testify of God's faithfulness, goodness, and deliverance in my life. I will not be silent, but I will declare His mighty works.
26. Heavenly Father, I ask for your angels to surround me and protect me from every spiritual attack. Let your angelic hosts be a wall of fire around me, repelling every evil force and keeping me safe in your presence, in the name of Jesus Christ.

27. I command every spirit of confusion, doubt, and unbelief to leave my mind and my heart. I receive the peace of God that surpasses all understanding, and I trust in His promises and faithfulness, in the name of Jesus Christ.
28. Lord, I surrender my will and my plans to you. Let your perfect will be done in my life, and let your kingdom come. I seek first your kingdom and your righteousness, knowing that all other things will be added unto me.
29. I break and renounce every curse or hex that has been spoken over me or my family. I declare that no weapon formed against us shall prosper, and every tongue that rises against us in judgment shall be condemned, in the name of Jesus Christ.
30. Heavenly Father, I ask for a fresh infilling of your Holy Spirit. Fill me to overflowing with your presence and power, and let your anointing destroy every yoke of bondage in my life, in the name of Jesus Christ.
31. I declare that I am a vessel of honor, sanctified and set apart for your purposes. I renounce every unclean spirit and every ungodly influence that has tried to defile my body, soul, or spirit, in the name of Jesus Christ.
32. Lord, I repent for any pride or self-reliance that has hindered my deliverance. I humble myself before you and acknowledge my complete dependence on your grace and mercy. Deliver me, Lord, and set me free, in the name of Jesus Christ.
33. I reject and renounce every spirit of rejection, abandonment, and worthlessness. I embrace my identity as a child of God, chosen and loved. I am accepted in the beloved, and I walk in the confidence of my true identity, in the name of Jesus Christ.
34. Heavenly Father, I ask for the baptism of your love to fill my heart. Let your love cast out all fear and heal every wound. I receive your love and extend it to others, breaking the cycle of hurt and bondage, in the name of Jesus Christ.

35. I declare that I am covered by the armor of God. I put on the belt of truth, the breastplate of righteousness, the shoes of the gospel of peace, the shield of faith, the helmet of salvation, and the sword of the Spirit, in the name of Jesus Christ.
36. Lord, I break every curse of failure and defeat that has hindered my progress. I declare that I am more than a conqueror through Christ Jesus, and I walk in victory and success in every area of my life, in the name of Jesus Christ.
37. I renounce and break any soul ties or emotional attachments that have kept me bound to unhealthy relationships or toxic patterns. I cut off every ungodly soul tie, and I release others to walk in their own freedom, in the name of Jesus Christ.
38. Heavenly Father, I ask for the power to forgive those who have hurt me deeply. Help me to release any bitterness, resentment, or desire for revenge. Set me free from the chains of unforgiveness and teach me to love as you love, in the name of Jesus Christ.
39. I declare that I am delivered from the power of darkness and transferred into the kingdom of light. I am no longer under the dominion of Satan but under the authority of Jesus Christ. His blood has set me free.
40. Lord, I break and sever every word curse that has been spoken over me or my family. I declare that we are blessed and highly favored by God. I cancel the effects of negative words and release the power of God's blessings, in the name of Jesus Christ.
41. I command every spirit of addiction and bondage to leave my life now, in the name of Jesus. I am free from the chains of addiction to drugs, alcohol, pornography, or any other destructive habit. I walk in the freedom and liberty of Christ.
42. Heavenly Father, I ask for your divine protection over my mind and my thoughts. Guard my mind from every lie and deception of the enemy. Let your truth reign in my thought life and bring

every thought captive to the obedience of Christ, in the name of Jesus Christ.
43. I declare that I am a co-heir with Christ, and I possess every spiritual blessing that is available to me. I am seated with Christ in heavenly places, far above all principalities and powers. I am more than a conqueror in Him.
44. Lord, I ask for your grace and strength to resist the temptations of the enemy. Give me the power to overcome every snare and trap set before me. I choose righteousness and holiness, and I reject every form of evil, in the name of Jesus Christ.
45. I release the fire of God to consume every demonic stronghold that has held me captive. Let the fire of God burn away every attachment and dependency on the enemy. I am free, in Jesus' name.
46. Heavenly Father, I ask for the restoration of every area of my life that has been damaged or destroyed by spiritual bondage. Bring healing and wholeness to my relationships, my finances, my health, and my emotions. Restore what the enemy has stolen, in the name of Jesus Christ.
47. I declare that I am filled with the power and authority of Jesus Christ. Every knee must bow, and every tongue confess that Jesus is Lord over my life. I walk in the victory that He has won for me on the cross.
48. Lord, I surrender my desires and ambitions to you. Align them with your perfect will and guide my steps. Let your plans and purposes prevail in my life, and let your glory be revealed through me, in the name of Jesus Christ.
49. I break and sever every ancestral curse and generational bondage in my bloodline. I declare that I am a new creation in Christ, and I am not bound by the sins or patterns of my ancestors. I am set free by the blood of Jesus.
50. Heavenly Father, I thank you for the deliverance and freedom that you have brought into my life. I walk in your victory, and

I testify of your goodness and faithfulness. I declare that I am delivered from every spiritual bondage, in Jesus' name. Amen.

DAY 3

Protection from Spiritual Attacks:
Divine Safeguard Against the Schemes of the Enemy

In the journey of life, we often encounter various challenges that test our faith, character, and resilience. While some difficulties may be physical or emotional in nature, there is another realm of battle that often goes unnoticed—the spiritual realm. Spiritual attacks are real, and they can manifest in subtle ways, seeking to keep us trapped in destructive patterns. However, as believers, we are not left defenseless. Divine protection equips us with the necessary tools to overcome these attacks and walk in victory. Today, we will explore how we can shield ourselves from spiritual attacks, relying on the power of God and His Word.

- Recognize the Existence of Spiritual Attacks:
  Ephesians 6:12 reminds us, *"For our struggle is not against flesh and blood, but against the rulers, against the authorities, against the powers of this dark world and against the spiritual forces of evil in the heavenly realms."* Acknowledging the reality of spiritual attacks is the first step in guarding ourselves against them.

- Clothe Yourself with Spiritual Armor:
  Ephesians 6:13-18 describes the spiritual armor that God provides for our protection. This armor includes the belt of truth, the breastplate of righteousness, the shoes of the gospel of peace, the shield of faith, the helmet of salvation, and the sword of the Spirit, which is the Word of God. By putting on

this armor daily through prayer and meditation on God's Word, we fortify ourselves against the enemy's schemes.

- Seek a Relationship with God:
Drawing close to God through prayer, worship, and regular study of the Scriptures deepens our connection with Him. James 4:7-8 encourages us to *"submit ourselves, then, to God. Resist the devil, and he will flee from you. Come near to God, and he will come near to you."* The more we commune with God, the more His divine protection surrounds us, making it harder for spiritual attacks to penetrate our lives.

- Employ the Power of God's Word:
The Bible is a powerful weapon against spiritual attacks. Hebrews 4:12 states, *"For the word of God is alive and active. Sharper than any double-edged sword, it penetrates even to dividing soul and spirit, joints and marrow; it judges the thoughts and attitudes of the heart."* By memorizing and meditating on God's Word, we gain strength, wisdom, and discernment to recognize and counter the enemy's lies and deceptions.

- Surround Yourself with Fellow Believers:
Ecclesiastes 4:12 says, *"Though one may be overpowered, two can defend themselves. A cord of three strands is not quickly broken."* Engaging in Christian community provides support, encouragement, and accountability. It is essential to connect with fellow believers who can pray for and with you, offer godly counsel, and stand in unity against spiritual attacks.

Spiritual attacks are a reality for believers, but we are not without protection. By recognizing the existence of these attacks, clothing us with the spiritual armor, seeking a close relationship with God, relying on His Word, and surrounding ourselves with fellow believers, we can withstand and overcome the schemes of the enemy. Remember, *"Greater is He who is in you than he who is in the world"* (1 John 4:4). With divine protection, we can confidently walk in victory and live out our God-given purpose.

Confession & Declaration:

In the name of Jesus, I declare that the powers of darkness operating against me are broken! According to Ephesians 6:12, *"For we do not wrestle against flesh and blood, but against the rulers, against the authorities, against the cosmic powers over this present darkness, against the spiritual forces of evil in the heavenly places."* I stand firm in the authority I have in Christ, and I rebuke every demonic force that seeks to hinder my progress and well-being.

I declare that I am a child of God, redeemed by the blood of Jesus. Romans 8:37 declares, *"No, in all these things we are more than conquerors through him who loved us."* I reject any power of darkness that tries to intimidate or oppress me, for I am more than a conqueror through Christ!

I declare that I am filled with the Holy Spirit and His power resides within me. 2 Timothy 1:7 assures me that *"God gave us a spirit not of fear but of power and love and self-control."* I reject fear and any stronghold of darkness, knowing that I have the power to overcome through the Spirit of God.

I declare that every curse spoken against me is nullified by the power of the cross. Galatians 3:13 says, *"Christ redeemed us from the curse of the law by becoming a curse for us."* I proclaim my freedom from every generational curse, every spoken curse, and every witchcraft attack. I am washed clean by the blood of Jesus.

I declare that I walk in the light of God's truth, and the lies of darkness have no power over me. Psalm 27:1 affirms, *"The Lord is my light and my salvation; whom shall I fear?"* I reject every lie, deception, and manipulation of the enemy. I stand on the truth of God's Word and declare victory over the powers of darkness.

I stand firm in these declarations, knowing that God's Word is powerful and cannot be broken, and that God is faithful to bring deliverance and victory in every area of my life. I trust in His promises and rest in His unfailing love.

Prayer of Deliverance

1. Heavenly Father, I thank you for your faithfulness and love towards me. I come before you today, seeking your divine protection against all spiritual attacks. (Psalm 91:2)
2. Lord, I declare that no weapon formed against me shall prosper, and every tongue that rises against me in judgment shall be condemned. I am protected by your righteousness. (Isaiah 54:17)
3. I cover myself with the armor of God— the belt of truth, the breastplate of righteousness, the shoes of the gospel of peace, the shield of faith, the helmet of salvation, and the sword of the Spirit— to withstand every spiritual attack. (Ephesians 6:13-17)
4. Father, I rebuke and bind every spirit of darkness and evil that is assigned to attack my life, my family, and my destiny. I command them to flee in the name of Jesus. (James 4:7)
5. Lord, I renounce and reject any ungodly alliances or agreements I have made consciously or unconsciously, which open doors for spiritual attacks. I break every unholy covenant by the blood of Jesus. (Proverbs 1:10)

6. Heavenly Father, I ask you to dispatch your mighty angels to surround me and protect me from all forms of spiritual attacks. Let them encamp around me and deliver me from all harm, in the name of Jesus Christ. (Psalm 34:7)
7. Lord, I declare that I am hidden in the secret place of the Most High, and I abide under the shadow of the Almighty. No evil shall befall me, and no plague shall come near my dwelling, in the name of Jesus Christ. (Psalm 91:1, 10)
8. I command every demonic assignment against my mind, emotions, and thoughts to be nullified in the name of Jesus. I take every thought captive and make it obedient to Christ. (2 Corinthians 10:5)
9. Father, I pray for discernment and spiritual wisdom to recognize and expose every scheme and tactic of the enemy. Open my eyes to see the traps set before me and guide me in the path of righteousness, in the name of Jesus Christ. (Ephesians 5:11)
10. Lord, I plead the blood of Jesus over every area of my life. Let the blood of Jesus be a covering that shields me from all spiritual attacks and renders the enemy powerless, in the name of Jesus Christ. (Revelation 12:11)
11. I declare that I am more than a conqueror through Christ Jesus. I am an overcomer, and no weapon formed against me shall prosper. (Romans 8:37)
12. Heavenly Father, I break and cancel every curse or spell that has been spoken or placed upon me. I release myself from the bondage of every generational curse and declare my freedom in Christ. (Galatians 3:13)
13. Lord, I pray for divine wisdom and discernment to navigate through spiritual warfare. Grant me insight into the strategies of the enemy and the ability to stand firm in your truth. (Colossians 2:8)

14. I renounce every ungodly soul tie and spiritual attachment that hinders my walk with you. I sever all ties with ungodly influences and submit myself wholly to your will, in the name of Jesus Christ. (1 Corinthians 6:17)
15. Father, I pray for divine protection over my physical health. Guard me against any sickness, disease, or infirmity that the enemy may try to bring upon me, in the name of Jesus Christ. (Psalm 91:10)
16. Lord, I pray for a hedge of protection around my loved ones. Guard them from every spiritual attack and keep them safe from all harm and danger, in the name of Jesus Christ. (Psalm 125:2)
17. I declare that no weapon formed against my finances and resources shall prosper. I am blessed and prospered by the hand of God. (Philippians 4:19)
18. Heavenly Father, I ask for supernatural discernment to recognize false teachings, doctrines, and manipulations of the enemy. Lead me in the paths of truth and righteousness. (1 John 4:1)
19. Lord, I rebuke and bind every spirit of fear, doubt, and discouragement. I declare that I have a sound mind, and I am filled with faith, courage, and hope in Christ Jesus. (2 Timothy 1:7)
20. I pray for the protection of my relationships. Guard them against division, strife, and any spiritual attack that seeks to destroy unity and love. (Ephesians 4:3)
21. Heavenly Father, I ask for your protection over my spiritual life. Shield me from deception, false prophets, and every hindrance that seeks to derail my relationship with you. (Matthew 24:4)
22. Lord, I pray for divine favor and protection in my workplace or business. Expose and thwart every plan of the enemy to hinder my success and advancement, in the name of Jesus Christ. (Psalm 5:12)

23. I break every curse of barrenness and unfruitfulness over my life. I declare that I am fruitful and multiply in every area of my life, according to God's plan and purpose. (Genesis 1:28)
24. Father, I ask for your protection over my dreams and visions. Guard them from spiritual attacks that aim to distort, distract, or discourage me from pursuing your plans for my life. (Acts 2:17)
25. Lord, I pray for divine protection over my time of prayer and intimacy with you. Shield me from distractions, spiritual dryness, and attacks that seek to hinder my communion with you. (Matthew 6:6)
26. I declare that I am covered by the fire of the Holy Spirit. Let every arrow of the enemy be consumed by the divine fire and let his schemes be exposed and destroyed, in the name of Jesus Christ. (Hebrews 12:29)
27. Heavenly Father, I pray for protection over my reputation and character. Guard me against false accusations, slander, and attacks that seek to damage my integrity, in the name of Jesus Christ. (Psalm 54:1)
28. Lord, I pray for divine guidance and protection in my decision-making. Help me to discern your will and purpose for my life and protect me from making choices that would lead me away from your plan, in the name of Jesus Christ. (Proverbs 3:5-6)
29. I declare that I am a child of God, and no weapon formed against me shall prosper. I am marked by the blood of Jesus and sealed by the Holy Spirit. (Ephesians 1:13-14)
30. Father, I pray for divine protection over my sleep and rest. Guard me against nightmares, night terrors, and any spiritual attacks that seek to disturb my peace, in the name of Jesus Christ. (Psalm 4:8)
31. Lord, I rebuke and bind every spirit of confusion and chaos that seeks to disrupt my life. I declare that I have the mind of Christ and walk in clarity, order, and peace. (1 Corinthians 14:33)

32. I pray for divine protection over my travels. Guide me safely to my destination and shield me from any accidents, incidents, or dangers along the way, in the name of Jesus Christ. (Psalm 121:8)
33. Heavenly Father, I ask for your protection over my emotions and feelings. Guard me against despair, depression, anxiety, and every attack that seeks to steal my joy and peace, in the name of Jesus Christ. (Philippians 4:7)
34. Lord, I pray for divine protection over my ministry and service to others. Guard me against burnout, spiritual attacks, and any obstacles that seek to hinder the work you have called me to do. (1 Corinthians 15:58)
35. I declare that no curse or evil spoken against me shall prosper, in the name of Jesus Christ. I am covered by the blessing and favor of God. (Numbers 23:23)
36. Heavenly Father, I pray for protection over my words and speech. Help me to speak life, truth, and encouragement, and guard me against gossip, slander, and negative speech, in the name of Jesus Christ. (Proverbs 18:21)
37. Lord, I pray for divine protection over my family and loved ones. Shield them from all harm, danger, and spiritual attacks. Cover them with your love and surround them with your angels. (Psalm 91:11-12)
38. I declare that I am victorious in Christ. No weapon formed against me shall prosper, and every tongue that rises against me in judgment shall be proven wrong, in the name of Jesus Christ. (Isaiah 54:17)
39. Heavenly Father, I ask for your protection over my dreams and aspirations. Guard them from discouragement, doubt, and attacks that seek to undermine my purpose and destiny, in the name of Jesus Christ. (Jeremiah 29:11)
40. Lord, I pray for divine protection over my children. Guard them physically, emotionally, and spiritually. Surround them with

your love and guide them in your ways, in the name of Jesus Christ. (Psalm 127:3)
41. I declare that I am covered by the blood of Jesus. Let every evil arrow, curse, or spell directed towards me be nullified and rendered powerless, in the name of Jesus Christ. (Revelation 12:11)
42. Heavenly Father, I ask for your protection over my faith. Strengthen me in times of doubt, protect me from spiritual attacks on my belief, and deepen my trust in you. (1 Peter 1:5)
43. Lord, I pray for divine protection over my obedience to your word. Guard me from compromise, disobedience, and every attack that seeks to divert me from following your commandments. (John 14:15)
44. I declare that no enchantment, divination, or witchcraft formed against me shall prevail. I am shielded by the power of God, in the name of Jesus Christ. (Numbers 23:23)
45. Heavenly Father, I pray for divine protection over my joy. Guard me against bitterness, unforgiveness, and every attack that seeks to steal my happiness in Christ. (Nehemiah 8:10)
46. Lord, I pray for divine protection over my spiritual gifts and talents. Guard me from comparison, self-doubt, and attacks that seek to hinder me from using them for your glory, in the name of Jesus Christ. (Romans 12:6)
47. I declare that I am anointed and empowered by the Holy Spirit. I am equipped to overcome every spiritual attack and walk in victory, in the name of Jesus Christ. (1 John 2:20)
48. Heavenly Father, I ask for your protection over my relationships with others. Guard them from discord, strife, and every attack that seeks to disrupt unity and love, in the name of Jesus Christ. (Colossians 3:14)
49. Lord, I pray for divine protection over my future and destiny. Guard me from distractions, detours, and attacks that seek to

hinder me from fulfilling your purpose for my life, in the name of Jesus Christ. (Jeremiah 29:11)
50. I declare that I am hidden in Christ, and no spiritual attack can separate me from your love. I am secure in your hands, and I trust in your unfailing protection, in the name of Jesus Christ. (Romans 8:38-39)

DAY 4

Renewing the Mind: Transforming Thinking Through God's Word

Our minds are powerful instruments that shape our perceptions, decisions, and actions. However, in a world filled with negativity and challenges, our minds can easily become cluttered with negative thoughts and beliefs. Fortunately, as believers, we have access to a divine source of renewal and transformation. By asking God to renew our minds and align our thinking with His truth, we can break free from the patterns of negativity and experience a renewed perspective on life. Today, we will explore the importance of renewing the mind and how it can be achieved through the power of Scripture.

- Recognizing the Need for Mind Renewal:
  In Romans 12:2, the apostle Paul urges us not to conform to the patterns of this world but to be transformed by the renewing of our minds. Our natural inclination may be to conform to the negative thinking patterns prevalent in society, leading to fear, doubt, and discouragement. However, God calls us to a higher standard, one that involves transforming our minds through His truth.

- Asking God for Mind Renewal:
  In Psalm 51:10, King David implores God, saying, *"Create in me a clean heart, O God, and renew a steadfast spirit within me."* Similarly, we can seek God's intervention in renewing our minds. By humbling ourselves before Him and inviting Him to

transform our thinking, we open the door for His divine work in our lives.

- Feeding on God's Word:
  Renewing our minds involves replacing negative thoughts and beliefs with the truth found in God's Word. In Joshua 1:8, God instructs Joshua, saying, *"This Book of the Law shall not depart from your mouth, but you shall meditate on it day and night, so that you may be careful to do according to all that is written in it."* Regularly immersing ourselves in Scripture allows us to align our thoughts with God's truth and develop a renewed perspective.

- Overcoming Negative Patterns:
  Negative thinking patterns can be deeply ingrained in our minds, making them difficult to break. However, with the power of God's Word, we can overcome them. Philippians 4:8 provides a guideline for transforming our thought patterns, instructing us to dwell on whatever is true, noble, right, pure, lovely, admirable, excellent, or praiseworthy. By deliberately focusing on these positive aspects, we can retrain our minds and break free from negativity.

- Embracing the Power of Prayer and Meditation:
  Prayer is a vital tool in the process of renewing the mind. We can pour out our hearts to God, asking Him to reveal areas in our thinking that need transformation. Additionally, meditation on Scripture enables us to internalize God's truth and allow it to shape our thoughts and beliefs. As Psalm 119:15 states, *"I meditate on your precepts and consider your ways."*

Renewing the mind is a transformative process that requires intentional effort and reliance on God's Word. By inviting God to renew our minds, we can break free from negative thought patterns and align our thinking with His truth. As we meditate on Scripture, pray, and consciously choose positive thoughts, we open ourselves to the transformative power of God. May we continually seek mind renewal, allowing God to shape our thoughts and transform our lives for His glory.

Confession & Declaration:

In the name of Jesus, I declare that the powers of darkness operating against me are broken! According to Ephesians 6:12, *"For we do not wrestle against flesh and blood, but against the rulers, against the authorities, against the cosmic powers over this present darkness, against the spiritual forces of evil in the heavenly places."* I stand firm in the authority I have in Christ, and I rebuke every demonic force that seeks to hinder my progress and well-being.

I declare that I am a child of God, redeemed by the blood of Jesus. Romans 8:37 declares, *"No, in all these things we are more than conquerors through him who loved us."* I reject any power of darkness that tries to intimidate or oppress me, for I am more than a conqueror through Christ!

I declare that I am filled with the Holy Spirit and His power resides within me. 2 Timothy 1:7 assures me that *"God gave us a spirit not of fear but of power and love and self-control."* I reject fear and any stronghold of darkness, knowing that I have the power to overcome through the Spirit of God.

I declare that every curse spoken against me is nullified by the power of the cross. Galatians 3:13 says, *"Christ redeemed us from the curse of the law by becoming a curse for us."* I proclaim my freedom from every generational curse, every spoken curse, and every witchcraft attack. I am washed clean by the blood of Jesus.

I declare that I walk in the light of God's truth, and the lies of darkness have no power over me. Psalm 27:1 affirms, *"The Lord is my light and my salvation; whom shall I fear?"* I reject every lie, deception, and manipulation of the enemy. I stand on the truth of God's Word and declare victory over the powers of darkness.

I stand firm in these declarations, knowing that God's Word is powerful and cannot be broken, and that God is faithful to bring deliverance and victory in every area of my life. I trust in His promises and rest in His unfailing love.

Prayer of Deliverance

1. Heavenly Father, I come before you today, asking for the renewal of my mind. Romans 12:2 reminds me to not conform to the patterns of this world but to be transformed by the renewing of my mind.
2. Lord, I declare that I will no longer be held captive by negative thoughts and beliefs. 2 Corinthians 10:5 teaches me to take every thought captive and make it obedient to Christ.
3. I break the stronghold of fear and anxiety over my mind in the name of Jesus. Philippians 4:6-7 assures me that with prayer and thanksgiving, your peace will guard my heart and mind.
4. Father, I renounce all thoughts of doubt and unbelief. Help me to trust in your promises and believe that all things are possible through Christ. Mark 9:23 reminds me that everything is possible for those who believe.
5. Lord, I reject the lies of the enemy and declare that I am fearfully and wonderfully made. Psalm 139:14 affirms that I am fearfully and wonderfully made by your hands.
6. I cast down every negative imagination and thought that exalts itself against the knowledge of God. 2 Corinthians 10:4-5

reminds me to demolish arguments and every pretension that sets itself up against the knowledge of God.
7. Heavenly Father, I surrender my thought life to you. Help me to focus on whatever is true, noble, right, pure, lovely, and admirable. Philippians 4:8 encourages me to dwell on these things.
8. I reject the spirit of bitterness and unforgiveness. Ephesians 4:31-32 reminds me to get rid of all bitterness, rage, anger, harsh words, and slander, and instead be kind and forgiving.
9. Lord, I ask for your wisdom and discernment to guide my thoughts and decisions. James 1:5 assures me that if I lack wisdom, I can ask you, and you will give it generously.
10. I break the power of negative self-talk and declare that I am a child of God, chosen and loved. 1 John 3:1 reminds me of the great love the Father has lavished upon me.
11. Heavenly Father, I surrender my worries and anxieties to you. 1 Peter 5:7 encourages me to cast all my cares upon you because you care for me.
12. I renounce the spirit of comparison and competition. Help me to embrace my uniqueness and celebrate the gifts and talents you have given me. 1 Corinthians 12:4-6 reminds me that there are different kinds of gifts, but the same Spirit.
13. Lord, I declare that I have a sound mind and that your perfect love casts out all fear. 2 Timothy 1:7 assures me that you have not given me a spirit of fear, but of power, love, and a sound mind.
14. I reject the lies of the enemy that tell me I am not worthy or valuable. Psalm 139:13 reminds me that you knit me together in my mother's womb and I am fearfully and wonderfully made.
15. Heavenly Father, I ask for your help in controlling my thoughts and aligning them with your truth. Proverbs 4:23 instructs me to guard my heart, for everything I do flows from it.

16. I break the power of negative memories and past traumas. Isaiah 43:18-19 reminds me that you are doing a new thing in my life, and I can forget the former things and move forward.
17. Lord, I surrender my desires and ambitions to you. Help me to seek your will above all else and trust that you will direct my paths. Proverbs 3:5-6 encourages me to trust in you with all my heart and lean not on my own understanding.
18. I renounce the spirit of pride and self-reliance. James 4:6 reminds me that you oppose the proud but give grace to the humble.
19. Heavenly Father, I ask for your help in renewing my mind daily through the reading and meditation of your Word. Psalm 119:105 assures me that your word is a lamp to my feet and a light to my path.
20. I break the power of negative influences and ungodly media in my life. Philippians 4:8 instructs me to focus on whatever is true, noble, right, pure, lovely, and admirable.
21. Lord, I declare that I have the mind of Christ. 1 Corinthians 2:16 assures me that I have the mind of Christ, and I can discern the things of the Spirit.
22. I reject the spirit of condemnation and embrace the forgiveness and grace you offer. Romans 8:1 reminds me that there is no condemnation for those who are in Christ Jesus.
23. Heavenly Father, I ask for your help in renewing my mind and breaking the patterns of negative thinking. Psalm 51:10 encourages me to create in me a pure heart and renew a steadfast spirit within me.
24. I renounce the spirit of hopelessness and despair. Romans 15:13 assures me that you are the God of hope, and you fill me with all joy and peace as I trust in you.
25. Lord, I ask for your strength to resist temptation and to take every thought captive to the obedience of Christ. 1 Corinthians

10:13 reminds me that you provide a way out when I am tempted.
26. I break the power of lies and deception over my mind. John 8:32 assures me that the truth will set me free.
27. Heavenly Father, I surrender my plans and desires to you. Help me to submit to your perfect will and trust that your plans are higher than mine. Proverbs 16:9 reminds me that a person's heart plans their way, but the Lord directs their steps.
28. I reject the spirit of doubt and choose to trust in your faithfulness. Hebrews 10:23 encourages me to hold unswervingly to the hope I profess, for you who promised are faithful.
29. Lord, I declare that I am more than a conqueror through Christ who loves me. Romans 8:37 assures me that in all things, I am more than a conqueror through him who loved me.
30. I renounce the spirit of negativity and complaining. Philippians 2:14 instructs me to do everything without grumbling or arguing.
31. Heavenly Father, I ask for your help in renewing my mind and transforming my thinking. Ephesians 4:23-24 encourages me to be renewed in the spirit of my mind and to put on the new self, created to be like you in true righteousness and holiness.
32. I break the power of guilt and shame over my mind. Psalm 103:12 assures me that as far as the east is from the west, so far you have removed my transgressions from me.
33. Lord, I declare that I am a new creation in Christ Jesus. 2 Corinthians 5:17 reminds me that if anyone is in Christ, they are a new creation; the old has gone, the new has come!
34. I reject the spirit of complacency and choose to pursue a deeper relationship with you. Matthew 6:33 instructs me to seek first your kingdom and your righteousness, and all these things will be added to me.

35. Heavenly Father, I ask for your help in renewing my mind and breaking the chains of addiction and destructive habits. Galatians 5:1 reminds me that it is for freedom that Christ has set me free.
36. I renounce the spirit of pride and self-centeredness. Philippians 2:3-4 instructs me to do nothing out of selfish ambition or vain conceit but to consider others better than myself.
37. Lord, I declare that I am loved and accepted by you. Ephesians 1:6 assures me that I am accepted in the Beloved.
38. I break the power of negative self-image and declare that I am fearfully and wonderfully made. Psalm 139:14 reminds me that I am fearfully and wonderfully made by your hands.
39. Heavenly Father, I ask for your help in renewing my mind and aligning my thoughts with your truth. John 17:17 teaches me that your word is truth.
40. I reject the spirit of discouragement and choose to put my hope in you. Psalm 42:11 reminds me to put my hope in you, for I will yet praise you, my Savior and my God.
41. Lord, I declare that I am more than enough in Christ. 2 Corinthians 3:5 assures me that my sufficiency is from you.
42. I renounce the spirit of self-condemnation and embrace your forgiveness and grace. Romans 8:1 reminds me that there is no condemnation for those who are in Christ Jesus.
43. Heavenly Father, I ask for your help in renewing my mind and breaking free from the bondage of negative thoughts. Psalm 23:3 assures me that you restore my soul and lead me in paths of righteousness.
44. I break the power of fear and embrace your perfect love. 1 John 4:18 reminds me that perfect love drives out fear.
45. Lord, I declare that I am a child of God, chosen and loved. 1 John 3:1 assures me that how great is the love the Father has lavished on me, that I should be called a child of God!

46. I reject the spirit of confusion and ask for your wisdom and guidance. James 1:5 encourages me to ask for wisdom, and you will give it generously.
47. Heavenly Father, I ask for your help in renewing my mind and transforming my thinking. Romans 12:2 instructs me to not be conformed to the patterns of this world but to be transformed by the renewing of my mind.
48. I renounce the spirit of defeat and embrace the victory I have in Christ. 1 Corinthians 15:57 assures me that thanks be to God, who gives us the victory through our Lord Jesus Christ!
49. Lord, I declare that I have a sound mind and self-control. 2 Timothy 1:7 reminds me that you have not given me a spirit of fear, but of power, love, and a sound mind.
50. I break the power of negative patterns of thinking and declare that I have the mind of Christ. 1 Corinthians 2:16 assures me that I have the mind of Christ, and I can discern the things of the Spirit.

DAY 5

Breaking Addictions:
Seek Freedom from Chains of Destructive Habits

Addictions can consume our lives, trapping us in an evil cycle of dependency and destruction. They rob us of our joy, freedom, and potential. However, there is hope! With the power of God's Word, we can find the strength and guidance needed to break free from any addiction or destructive habit that has kept us bound. Today, we will explore some scripture references that inspire and empower us on this journey towards liberation.

- Acknowledge the Problem:
  "Submit yourselves, then, to God. Resist the devil, and he will flee from you." (James 4:7)
  The first step in breaking free from addiction is to recognize its hold on us and admit our powerlessness. Surrendering to God and resisting the temptations of the enemy open the door to transformation and healing.

- Seek God's Help:
  "I can do all things through Christ who strengthens me." (Philippians 4:13)
  Breaking addiction requires supernatural strength. Turning to God in prayer and seeking His guidance and support enables us to tap into His limitless power, which equips us to overcome even the toughest challenges.

- Renew Your Mind:

"Do not conform to the pattern of this world but be transformed by the renewing of your mind. Then you will be able to test and approve what God's will is—his good, pleasing and perfect will." (Romans 12:2)

To break free from destructive habits, we must change our thought patterns and align them with God's truth. Regularly immersing ourselves in His Word, meditating on His promises, and surrounding ourselves with positive influences can help us overcome negative thinking and find lasting freedom.

- Replace with Good Habits:
  "Do not be overcome by evil but overcome evil with good." (Romans 12:21)
  Breaking an addiction involves replacing unhealthy behaviors with positive ones. Engaging in activities that promote spiritual, mental, and physical well-being not only helps us overcome temptation but also leads to personal growth and fulfillment.

- Find Support:
  "Two are better than one, because they have a good return for their labor: If either of them falls down, one can help the other up." (Ecclesiastes 4:9-10)
  Seeking support from trusted friends, family, or a faith-based community can provide the encouragement, accountability, and guidance needed during the recovery process. Surrounding ourselves with like-minded individuals who share our commitment to breaking free strengthens our resolve and fosters a supportive environment.

Breaking addictions and destructive habits is a challenging journey, but with God's help and the power of His Word, we can find true freedom. Remember, the process may not be instant, and setbacks may occur, but do not lose heart. God's grace is sufficient, and His strength is made perfect in our weakness. As we submit to His will and lean on His promises, we can break the chains that bind us, experiencing a life of joy, purpose, and lasting freedom in Christ.

Confession & Declaration:

In the name of Jesus, I declare that the powers of darkness operating against me are broken! According to Ephesians 6:12, *"For we do not wrestle against flesh and blood, but against the rulers, against the authorities, against the cosmic powers over this present darkness, against the spiritual forces of evil in the heavenly places."* I stand firm in the authority I have in Christ, and I rebuke every demonic force that seeks to hinder my progress and well-being.

I declare that I am a child of God, redeemed by the blood of Jesus. Romans 8:37 declares, *"No, in all these things we are more than conquerors through him who loved us."* I reject any power of darkness that tries to intimidate or oppress me, for I am more than a conqueror through Christ!

I declare that I am filled with the Holy Spirit and His power resides within me. 2 Timothy 1:7 assures me that *"God gave us a spirit not of fear but of power and love and self-control."* I reject fear and any stronghold of darkness, knowing that I have the power to overcome through the Spirit of God.

I declare that every curse spoken against me is nullified by the power of the cross. Galatians 3:13 says, *"Christ redeemed us from the curse of the law by becoming a curse for us."* I proclaim my freedom from every generational curse, every spoken curse, and every witchcraft attack. I am washed clean by the blood of Jesus.

I declare that I walk in the light of God's truth, and the lies of darkness have no power over me. Psalm 27:1 affirms, *"The Lord is my light and my salvation; whom shall I fear?"* I reject every lie, deception, and manipulation of the enemy. I stand on the truth of God's Word and declare victory over the powers of darkness.

I stand firm in these declarations, knowing that God's Word is powerful and cannot be broken, and that God is faithful to bring deliverance and victory in every area of my life. I trust in His promises and rest in His unfailing love.

Prayer of Deliverance

1. Heavenly Father, I come before you seeking freedom from addiction. Your Word assures me in Romans 6:18 that I have been set free from sin and have become a slave to righteousness. Grant me the strength to break free from the chains of addiction and walk in the freedom you have provided, in the name of Jesus Christ.
2. Lord, I declare that I am more than a conqueror through Christ who loves me (Romans 8:37). I renounce any power addiction has had over my life and choose to walk in victory, in the name of Jesus Christ.
3. O God my Father, I surrender my addiction to you, for your Word says in Matthew 11:28, *"Come to me, all you who are weary and burdened, and I will give you rest."* I receive your rest and release from the bondage of addiction.
4. Heavenly Father, I declare that I am a new creation in Christ (2 Corinthians 5:17). I choose to leave behind the old patterns of addiction and embrace the new life you have given me.
5. Lord, I seek your strength to resist temptation and overcome cravings. Your Word promises in 1 Corinthians 10:13 that You

will provide a way out. I trust in Your faithfulness and power to deliver me from all forms of addiction.

6. God, I acknowledge that my body is a temple of the Holy Spirit (1 Corinthians 6:19). I commit to treating it with respect and honoring you by breaking free from any addictive substances or behaviors, in the name of Jesus Christ.
7. Heavenly Father, I declare that I am rooted and grounded in your love (Ephesians 3:17). Your love gives me the strength to say no to the allure of addiction and choose a life of purity and freedom.
8. Lord, I renounce the lies and deceit of the enemy. Your Word declares in John 8:32 that the truth will set me free. I choose to meditate on your truth and reject the lies that fuel addiction.
9. God, I pray for a renewed mind (Romans 12:2). Help me to think thoughts that are pure, noble, and praiseworthy. Let my mind be focused on your goodness and truth rather than the allure of addiction.
10. Heavenly Father, I ask for accountability and support from fellow believers. Your Word tells us in Ecclesiastes 4:9-10 that two are better than one. Surround me with godly friends who will encourage me on this journey of breaking addiction.
11. Lord, I declare that I am filled with your Spirit (Ephesians 5:18). I choose to walk in the Spirit and not fulfill the desires of the flesh. Fill me afresh with your Spirit and empower me to overcome addiction.
12. God, I pray for healing from the wounds and hurts that may have contributed to my addiction. Your Word says in Psalm 147:3 that you heal the brokenhearted and bind up their wounds. Heal me, Lord, and set me free from the emotional pain that has fueled my addiction, in the name of Jesus Christ.
13. Heavenly Father, I declare that I am dead to sin and alive to righteousness (Romans 6:11). I choose to live a life that honors you, free from the chains of addiction.

14. Lord, I thank you for the power of your Word. Your Word is a lamp to my feet and a light to my path (Psalm 119:105). Guide me, Lord, as I navigate the path of breaking addiction, and help me to find strength and encouragement in your Word.
15. God, I pray for divine strength to resist triggers and avoid situations that may lead to temptation. Your Word assures me in 1 Corinthians 15:57 that I have victory through Jesus Christ. Strengthen me, Lord, to walk in that victory.
16. Heavenly Father, I choose to take every thought captive to the obedience of Christ (2 Corinthians 10:5). Help me to reject thoughts of addiction and instead fix my mind on you and your promises.
17. Lord, I declare that I am an overcomer by the blood of the Lamb and the word of my testimony (Revelation 12:11). I testify to your power to break addictions and declare my freedom in Christ.
18. God, I pray for wisdom and discernment to make choices that align with your will. Your Word promises in James 1:5 that if anyone lacks wisdom, they should ask you, and you will give it generously. Grant me wisdom, Lord, to make choices that lead me away from addiction, in the name of Jesus Christ.
19. Heavenly Father, I declare that I am more than enough in Christ. Your Word assures me in Philippians 4:13 that I can do all things through Christ who strengthens me. I am empowered to break free from addiction and walk in victory.
20. Lord, I renounce the spirit of addiction and declare that my body is under the control of the Holy Spirit. Your Word tells me in 1 Corinthians 6:12 that I will not be mastered by anything. I choose to yield to the Holy Spirit's control and break free from addiction's grip, in the name of Jesus Christ.
21. God, I pray for restoration and wholeness in every area of my life. Your Word promises in Joel 2:25 that you will restore what

the locusts have eaten. I trust in your faithfulness to restore me and set me free from addiction.

22. Heavenly Father, I declare that I am strong in the Lord and in the power of His might (Ephesians 6:10). I am not weak and helpless against addiction but am empowered by your Spirit to overcome.

23. Lord, I surrender my cravings and desires to you. Your Word tells me in Psalm 37:4 that when I delight myself in you, you will give me the desires of my heart. Help me to find true satisfaction and fulfillment in you rather than seeking it through addictive substances or behaviors, in the name of Jesus Christ.

24. O God my Father, I pray for perseverance and endurance on this journey of breaking addiction. Your Word encourages me in James 1:12 that those who persevere under trial will receive the crown of life. Strengthen me, Lord, to endure and press on toward the freedom you have promised.

25. Heavenly Father, I declare that I am no longer a slave to sin but a servant of righteousness (Romans 6:22). I choose to serve you wholeheartedly and break free from the bondage of addiction.

26. O Lord, I ask for forgiveness for any harm I have caused myself or others due to my addiction. Your Word assures me in 1 John 1:9 that if I confess my sins, you are faithful and just to forgive me. I receive your forgiveness and choose to walk in freedom.

27. O God my Father, I pray for emotional healing and restoration. Your Word promises in Isaiah 61:3 that you will give beauty for ashes and the oil of joy for mourning. Heal my heart, Lord, and replace the void that addiction has left with your joy and peace.

28. Heavenly Father, I declare that I am an ambassador of Christ (2 Corinthians 5:20). Help me to represent you well by breaking free from addiction and living a life that reflects your love and grace.

29. O Lord, I pray for divine strength in moments of weakness and vulnerability. Your Word tells me in Psalm 46:1 that you are my

refuge and strength, a very present help in trouble. I lean on you for strength and find refuge in your presence, in the name of Jesus Christ.

30. O Lord, I thank you for the victory I have in Christ. Your Word assures me in 1 John 5:4 that whatever is born of God overcomes the world. I am born of God, and I overcome addiction through the power of Jesus Christ.

31. Heavenly Father, I choose to forgive myself for past mistakes and failures. Your Word teaches me in Psalm 103:12 that you have removed my sins as far as the east is from the west. Help me to walk in the freedom of your forgiveness and let go of guilt and shame.

32. Lord, I pray for a renewed passion and zeal for you. Your Word says in Psalm 37:4 that when I delight myself in you, you will give me the desires of my heart. Ignite a burning desire within me to pursue you wholeheartedly and find fulfillment in you alone.

33. God, I surrender my will to yours. Your Word encourages me in Proverbs 3:5-6 to trust in you with all my heart and lean not on my own understanding. Direct my steps, Lord, and help me to align my will with yours as I seek freedom from addiction.

34. Heavenly Father, I declare that I am set apart for your purposes. Your Word tells me in 1 Peter 2:9 that I am a chosen generation, a royal priesthood. I renounce the influence of addiction and embrace my identity as your child, called to a life of freedom and purpose.

35. O Lord, I pray for a renewed sense of self-worth and identity in Christ. Your Word assures me in Psalm 139:14 that I am fearfully and wonderfully made. Help me to see myself through your eyes and break free from any self-destructive behaviors associated with addiction, in the name of Jesus Christ.

36. God, I declare that I am an heir of God and a joint heir with Christ (Romans 8:17). I renounce any addiction that has sought

to rob me of my inheritance in Christ and choose to walk in the fullness of all you have for me, in the name of Jesus Christ.

37. Heavenly Father, I declare that I am clothed with the armor of God (Ephesians 6:11). Help me to stand firm against the schemes of the enemy and break free from the strongholds of addiction.
38. Lord, I surrender my weaknesses to you, for your Word says in 2 Corinthians 12:9 that your grace is sufficient for me, and your power is made perfect in weakness. Strengthen me, Lord, in my moments of weakness and empower me to overcome addiction.
39. God, I pray for restoration of broken relationships caused by addiction. Your Word encourages me in Joel 2:25 that you can restore what has been lost. Heal the wounds caused by my addiction and bring reconciliation and healing to my relationships.
40. Heavenly Father, I choose to fill my mind with things that are pure and honorable (Philippians 4:8). Help me to guard my thoughts and focus on your truth rather than the destructive patterns of addiction.
41. Lord, I declare that I am set free by the truth of your Word. Your Word declares in John 8:36 that if the Son sets me free, I am free indeed. I receive the freedom you offer and renounce the bondage of addiction.
42. O God my Father, I pray for strength to resist peer pressure and the influence of others who may enable or encourage addictive behaviors. Your Word tells me in Proverbs 13:20 that I am influenced by those I surround myself with. Surround me with godly influences, Lord, and help me to make choices that honor you, in the name of Jesus Christ.
43. Heavenly Father, I declare that I am a temple of the Holy Spirit (1 Corinthians 6:19). I renounce any addiction that has defiled this temple and choose to honor you with my body, mind, and spirit.

44. Lord, I pray for discernment to recognize the root causes of my addiction. Your Word tells me in Psalm 139:23-24 to search my heart and reveal any offensive way in me. Shine your light on the deep places of my heart, Lord, and help me to address the underlying issues that contribute to addiction.
45. God, I pray for divine opportunities to share my testimony of freedom from addiction and bring hope to others who are struggling. Your Word tells me in 2 Corinthians 1:4 that you comfort us in all our affliction so that we may be able to comfort others. Use my story, Lord, to bring healing and freedom to those who are bound by addiction, in the name of Jesus Christ.
46. Heavenly Father, I declare that I am an overcomer in every area of my life, including addiction. Your Word assures me in Revelation 21:7 that the one who overcomes will inherit all things. I am an overcomer, and I receive the inheritance of freedom and abundant life in Christ.
47. O Lord, I pray for supernatural strength to resist the pull of addiction. Your Word tells me in Isaiah 40:29 that you give power to the weak and strength to the powerless. I rely on your strength, Lord, to break free and walk in victory.
48. O God my Father, I surrender my desires to you and ask that you align them with your will. Your Word encourages me in Psalm 37:4 that when I delight myself in you, you will give me the desires of my heart. Transform my desires, Lord, and help me to find satisfaction in you alone.
49. Heavenly Father, I declare that I am chosen, holy, and dearly loved by you (Colossians 3:12). I renounce any addiction that has sought to define or control me and embrace my true identity in Christ.
50. O Lord, I thank you for the freedom I have in Christ. Your Word assures me in Galatians 5:1 that it is for freedom that Christ has set me free. I receive and walk in that freedom, breaking every chain of addiction in Jesus' name. Amen.

DAY 6

Healing from Emotional Wounds: Walking in Wholeness and Restoration

Emotional wounds are a universal part of the human experience. We all encounter pain, loss, and disappointments that can deeply impact our hearts and minds. However, the journey towards healing is possible, and it leads us to a place of wholeness and restoration. Today, we will explore the path to emotional healing, drawing inspiration from timeless scripture references that offer comfort, guidance, and hope.

- Acknowledge the Pain:
  The first step towards healing is acknowledging the pain we carry. It's crucial to allow ourselves to grieve and process our emotions honestly. The Bible reminds us in Psalm 34:18, *"The Lord is near to the brokenhearted and saves the crushed in spirit."* Knowing that God is close to us in our pain provides solace and reassurance that we are not alone.

- Surrender to God:
  To experience true healing, we must surrender our wounds to God, trusting Him to bring restoration. In Jeremiah 29:11, God says, *"For I know the plans I have for you, declares the Lord, plans for welfare and not for evil, to give you a future and a hope."* Surrendering to God's plans means releasing our pain, bitterness, and resentment, allowing Him to work in us and through us.

- Seek Support:

Healing doesn't happen in isolation. Reach out for support from trusted friends, family, or professionals who can provide encouragement and guidance. Ecclesiastes 4:9-10 says, *"Two are better than one because they have a good reward for their toil. For if they fall, one will lift up his fellow. But woe to him who is alone when he falls and has not another to lift him up!"* The journey becomes easier when we have companions who can walk alongside us.

- Embrace Forgiveness:
Unforgiveness can hinder our healing journey and keep us trapped in a cycle of pain. Choose to forgive those who have hurt you, just as God forgives us. Colossians 3:13 reminds us, *"Bear with each other and forgive one another if any of you has a grievance against someone. Forgive as the Lord forgave you."* Forgiveness sets us free, releasing the burden of carrying grudges and allowing us to move forward in healing.

- Renew Your Mind:
Our thought patterns and beliefs greatly influence our emotional well-being. To experience healing, we must renew our minds with truth. Romans 12:2 encourages us, *"Do not be conformed to this world, but be transformed by the renewal of your mind, that by testing you may discern what is the will of God, what is good and acceptable and perfect."* Replace negative thoughts with God's promises and affirmations of His love and faithfulness.

- Find Purpose in Pain:
God can use our pain for a greater purpose. Joseph, in Genesis 50:20, declared, *"As for you, you meant evil against me, but God meant it for good, to bring it about that many people should be kept alive, as they are today."* Our wounds can

become a testimony of God's redeeming power and a source of comfort and encouragement to others who may be going through similar struggles.

Healing from emotional wounds is a transformative journey that requires patience, faith, and surrender. By acknowledging our pain, surrendering to God, seeking support, embracing forgiveness, renewing our minds, and finding purpose in our pain, we can experience wholeness and restoration. Let us hold onto God's promises and allow His love to heal the broken places within us. As we walk in healing, we become vessels of hope, sharing God's grace with others on their own journey towards emotional restoration.

Confession & Declaration:

In the name of Jesus, I declare that the powers of darkness operating against me are broken! According to Ephesians 6:12, *"For we do not wrestle against flesh and blood, but against the rulers, against the authorities, against the cosmic powers over this present darkness, against the spiritual forces of evil in the heavenly places."* I stand firm in the authority I have in Christ, and I rebuke every demonic force that seeks to hinder my progress and well-being.

I declare that I am a child of God, redeemed by the blood of Jesus. Romans 8:37 declares, *"No, in all these things we are more than conquerors through him who loved us."* I reject any power of darkness that tries to intimidate or oppress me, for I am more than a conqueror through Christ!

I declare that I am filled with the Holy Spirit and His power resides within me. 2 Timothy 1:7 assures me that *"God gave us a spirit not of fear but of power and love and self-control."* I reject fear and any stronghold of darkness, knowing that I have the power to overcome through the Spirit of God.

I declare that every curse spoken against me is nullified by the power of the cross. Galatians 3:13 says, *"Christ redeemed us from the curse of the law by becoming a curse for us."* I proclaim my freedom from every generational curse, every spoken curse, and every witchcraft attack. I am washed clean by the blood of Jesus.

I declare that I walk in the light of God's truth, and the lies of darkness have no power over me. Psalm 27:1 affirms, *"The Lord is my light and my salvation; whom shall I fear?"* I reject every lie, deception, and manipulation of the enemy. I stand on the truth of God's Word and declare victory over the powers of darkness.

I stand firm in these declarations, knowing that God's Word is powerful and cannot be broken, and that God is faithful to bring deliverance and victory in every area of my life. I trust in His promises and rest in His unfailing love.

Prayer of Deliverance

1. Heavenly Father, I come before you, seeking healing from emotional wounds that have left me broken and hurting. (Psalm 34:18)
2. O Lord my Father, let your love and compassion mend my shattered heart and bring restoration to my soul, in the name of Jesus Christ. (Psalm 147:3)
3. I release forgiveness to those who have caused me pain, knowing that forgiveness is a key to my own healing and freedom. (Colossians 3:13)

4. I renounce the lies and negative beliefs that have held me captive, and I choose to embrace the truth of your Word, which brings healing and transformation. (John 8:32)
5. Heavenly Father, I surrender my pain and sorrow to you, trusting that you will turn my mourning into joy and give me beauty for ashes, in the name of Jesus Christ. (Isaiah 61:3)
6. I declare that I am a new creation in Christ, and the old wounds and hurts no longer define me. I am being transformed into His image day by day. (2 Corinthians 5:17)
7. O Lord, I receive your comfort and peace in the midst of my pain. Your presence brings healing to my wounded heart, in the name of Jesus Christ. (Psalm 147:3)
8. I declare that I am fearfully and wonderfully made, and my worth is not determined by the opinions or actions of others. (Psalm 139:14)
9. Heavenly Father, I ask for your healing touch to restore my brokenness and bring wholeness to every area of my life, in the name of Jesus Christ. (Jeremiah 17:14)
10. I release any bitterness, resentment, or anger that I have been holding onto. I choose to walk in forgiveness and extend grace to myself and others. (Ephesians 4:31-32)
11. O Lord, I ask for your wisdom and discernment to navigate through the healing process. Guide me in choosing healthy relationships and making wise decisions for my emotional well-being. (James 1:5)
12. I declare that my past does not define my future. I am stepping into a season of restoration and victory, leaving behind the pain and embracing the promises you have for me, in the name of Jesus Christ. (Joel 2:25)
13. I choose to cast my anxieties on you, Lord, knowing that you care for me and will sustain me through every trial. (1 Peter 5:7)

14. Heavenly Father, I surrender my need for control and perfectionism. Help me to trust in your perfect plan for my life and find peace in surrendering to your will. (Proverbs 3:5-6)
15. I declare that I am an overcomer through Christ who strengthens me. I will not be defined by my past wounds but by the victory I have in Him, in the name of Jesus Christ. (Romans 8:37)
16. O Lord my Father, let your healing touch mend the broken relationships in my life. Restore what has been lost and bring reconciliation and harmony, in the name of Jesus Christ. (Matthew 5:9)
17. I declare that I am surrounded by your love and that your love drives out all fear and insecurity, in the name of Jesus Christ. (1 John 4:18)
18. Heavenly Father, I release any shame or guilt that I have carried from past mistakes. Your grace is sufficient for me, and I am forgiven and set free. (1 John 1:9)
19. I declare that I am filled with your joy and peace, which surpass all understanding. My emotions are anchored in your truth and goodness. (Romans 15:13)
20. O Lord, I surrender my need for approval from others. I find my worth and identity in you alone, and I am accepted and loved by you unconditionally. (Galatians 1:10)
21. I declare that I am a vessel of your love and healing. Use my story and my journey to bring hope and encouragement to others who are also wounded, in the name of Jesus Christ. (2 Corinthians 1:3-4)
22. Heavenly Father, let your Holy Spirit fill me afresh and empower me to walk in emotional wholeness and restoration, in the name of Jesus Christ. (Ephesians 5:18)
23. I declare that my mind is being renewed by the truth of your Word. I am letting go of negative thought patterns and embracing a mindset of hope and faith. (Romans 12:2)

24. O Lord, I surrender my need for control and surrender to your perfect timing in my healing process. I trust that you will bring about complete restoration in your perfect way. (Psalm 31:15)
25. I declare that I am a beloved child of God, and no emotional wound can separate me from your love. (Romans 8:38-39)
26. Heavenly Father, let divine wisdom and discernment identify and address any unhealthy patterns or behaviors that have contributed to my emotional wounds, in the name of Jesus Christ. (Proverbs 2:6)
27. I release any bitterness or resentment towards myself. I choose to embrace self-compassion and extend grace and forgiveness to myself, in the name of Jesus Christ. (Ephesians 4:32)
28. O Lord, let your supernatural peace guard my heart and mind, protecting me from anxiety and worry, in the name of Jesus Christ. (Philippians 4:7)
29. I declare that my identity is found in Christ alone. I am not defined by my past wounds or failures but by His love and grace. (Galatians 2:20)
30. Heavenly Father, I surrender my need to please others and seek their validation. I find my worth and affirmation in you, and Your opinion of me is what matters most. (Proverbs 29:25)
31. I declare that I am a temple of the Holy Spirit, and His presence brings healing and restoration to every part of my being. (1 Corinthians 6:19)
32. Almighty God, let your grace and mercy extend forgiveness and reconciliation to those who have wounded me, knowing that forgiveness brings freedom, in the name of Jesus Christ. (Matthew 6:14-15)
33. I declare that I am free from the chains of fear and insecurity. I am confident in who I am in Christ and walk in His perfect love. (1 John 4:16)

34. Almighty Father, I ask for your strength and perseverance to press on in my healing journey, even when it feels difficult or overwhelming, in the name of Jesus Christ. (Isaiah 40:31)
35. I declare that I am an instrument of peace. Where there is brokenness, I will bring healing. Where there is hurt, I will bring comfort. (Matthew 5:9)
36. O Lord, I surrender my need to understand everything and trust in your higher ways. Your ways are perfect, and you are working all things for my good. (Isaiah 55:8-9)
37. I declare that I am not alone in my healing process. You, Lord, are with me every step of the way, guiding and strengthening me, in the name of Jesus Christ. (Isaiah 41:10)
38. Heavenly Father, grant me supernatural restoration in my dreams and desires. Renew my hope and give me a vision for the future you have for me, in the name of Jesus Christ. (Jeremiah 29:11)
39. I release any bitterness or anger towards you, Lord, for allowing the wounds in my life. I trust that you will use them for my good and your glory. (Romans 8:28)
40. I declare that my emotions are under the control of the Holy Spirit. I am not ruled by fear, anger, or sadness, but by peace, joy, and love. (Galatians 5:22-23)
41. O Lord, grant me divine guidance in seeking professional help and counseling if needed. Surround me with wise and compassionate individuals who will support me on my journey to healing. (Proverbs 11:14)
42. I declare that I am an overcomer by the blood of the Lamb and the word of my testimony. My story will bring hope and healing to others. (Revelation 12:11)
43. Almighty Father, grant me grace to let go of the past and embrace the present moment. Help me to live fully in the present and not be bound by past hurts, in the name of Jesus Christ. (Philippians 3:13-14)

44. I declare that I am no longer a victim of my circumstances, but a victor through Christ who strengthens me. (1 Corinthians 15:57)
45. O Lord, I surrender my need to numb my pain through unhealthy coping mechanisms. Fill me with your presence and help me find healthy ways to process and heal, in the name of Jesus Christ. (Psalm 139:23-24)
46. I declare that I am anointed with the oil of joy and the garment of praise. My mourning will be turned into dancing and my sorrow into joy, in the name of Jesus Christ. (Psalm 30:11)
47. Heavenly Father, grant me grace to extend kindness and compassion to myself as I walk through the healing process. Help me to be patient and gentle with myself, in the name of Jesus Christ. (Ephesians 4:32)
48. I declare that I am set free from the bondage of shame and guilt. Your grace has washed me clean, and I am a new creation in Christ. (2 Corinthians 5:17)
49. O Lord, grant me wisdom to set healthy boundaries in my relationships, protecting myself from further emotional harm. Guide me in cultivating healthy and nurturing connections, in the name of Jesus Christ. (Proverbs 4:23)
50. I declare that your healing power is at work in my life. I will rise above my wounds and walk in wholeness, radiating your love and restoration to the world around me. (Psalm 107:20)

DAY 7

Breaking Financial Struggles: Experience Abundance and Provision

In today's world, many people find themselves facing financial struggles and the stress that comes with it. Whether it's mounting debt, unemployment, or unexpected expenses, the challenges can seem overwhelming. However, as we navigate these difficulties, it's important to remember that there is hope and divine provision available to us. Today, we will explore how scriptures can guide us towards experiencing abundance and provision, even in the midst of financial struggles.

- Trust in God's Faithfulness:
  Proverbs 3:5-6 (NIV) says, *"Trust in the Lord with all your heart and lean not on your own understanding; in all your ways submit to him, and he will make your paths straight."* By placing our trust in God and surrendering our financial concerns to Him, we can find peace and assurance that He will guide us towards financial stability.

- Seek First the Kingdom of God:
  Matthew 6:33 (NIV) reminds us, *"But seek first his kingdom and his righteousness, and all these things will be given to you as well."* When we prioritize our relationship with God and seek His will above all else, He promises to provide for our needs. By aligning our financial decisions and goals with God's principles, we can experience His abundant provision.

- Practice Faithful Stewardship:
  Luke 16:10 (NIV) teaches us, *"Whoever can be trusted with very little can also be trusted with much..."* It is crucial to manage our resources wisely, regardless of the amount we possess. By being faithful stewards of what we have, whether it's through budgeting, saving, or giving, we demonstrate our trustworthiness to God. In turn, He blesses us with more and increases our capacity to impact others positively.

- Generosity Reaps Blessings:
  2 Corinthians 9:6 (NIV) states, *"Remember this: Whoever sows sparingly will also reap sparingly, and whoever sows generously will also reap generously."* Even in times of financial struggle, cultivating a generous spirit can bring unexpected blessings. As we give with a cheerful heart, God honors our generosity and opens doors for provision to flow into our lives.

- Prayer and Faith:
  Philippians 4:6-7 (NIV) encourages us, *"Do not be anxious about anything, but in every situation, by prayer and petition, with thanksgiving, present your requests to God. And the peace of God, which transcends all understanding, will guard your hearts and your minds in Christ Jesus."* In times of financial stress, turning to God in prayer and placing our burdens before Him brings peace and comfort. Trusting in His timing and provision, our faith is strengthened, and breakthroughs can occur.

Financial struggles can be a challenging and stressful part of life, but as believers, we have the assurance that God is with us, providing for our needs. By trusting in His faithfulness, seeking His kingdom first, practicing faithful stewardship, cultivating a generous spirit, and relying on prayer and faith, we can experience abundance and provision, even in the midst of financial difficulties. Let us hold on to these scriptural truths and be confident that God's promises will never fail us.

Confession & Declaration:

In the name of Jesus, I declare that the powers of darkness operating against me are broken! According to Ephesians 6:12, *"For we do not wrestle against flesh and blood, but against the rulers, against the authorities, against the cosmic powers over this present darkness, against the spiritual forces of evil in the heavenly places."* I stand firm in the authority I have in Christ, and I rebuke every demonic force that seeks to hinder my progress and well-being.

I declare that I am a child of God, redeemed by the blood of Jesus. Romans 8:37 declares, *"No, in all these things we are more than conquerors through him who loved us."* I reject any power of darkness that tries to intimidate or oppress me, for I am more than a conqueror through Christ!

I declare that I am filled with the Holy Spirit and His power resides within me. 2 Timothy 1:7 assures me that *"God gave us a spirit not of fear but of power and love and self-control."* I reject fear and any stronghold of darkness, knowing that I have the power to overcome through the Spirit of God.

I declare that every curse spoken against me is nullified by the power of the cross. Galatians 3:13 says, *"Christ redeemed us from the curse of the law by becoming a curse for us."* I proclaim my freedom from every generational curse, every spoken curse, and every witchcraft attack. I am washed clean by the blood of Jesus.

I declare that I walk in the light of God's truth, and the lies of darkness have no power over me. Psalm 27:1 affirms, *"The Lord is my light and my salvation; whom shall I fear?"* I reject every lie, deception, and manipulation of the enemy. I stand on the truth of God's Word and declare victory over the powers of darkness.

I stand firm in these declarations, knowing that God's Word is powerful and cannot be broken, and that God is faithful to bring deliverance and victory in every area of my life. I trust in His promises and rest in His unfailing love.

Prayer of Deliverance

1. Heavenly Father, I declare that you are my provider and that you will break every financial struggle in my life. (Philippians 4:19)
2. Lord, I thank you for the abundance that is coming my way, as I trust in your promises and seek your kingdom first. (Matthew 6:33)
3. I declare that I am blessed to be a blessing, and I will experience overflow in every area of my finances, in the name of Jesus Christ. (Malachi 3:10)
4. Heavenly Father, I reject the spirit of poverty and lack in my life and declare that I am a child of the King, destined for prosperity, in the name of Jesus Christ. (Deuteronomy 8:18)
5. I declare that every debt in my life will be supernaturally canceled, and I will walk in financial freedom. (Psalm 37:21)
6. O Lord, I thank you for giving me wisdom and understanding to make sound financial decisions that will lead to abundance. (Proverbs 3:13-14)
7. I declare that my needs are met according to your riches in glory, and I will lack nothing, in the name of Jesus Christ. (Philippians 4:19)

8. Heavenly Father, I release any fear or worry about my financial situation and trust in your divine provision. (Matthew 6:25-27)
9. I declare that I am a good steward of the resources you have entrusted to me, and I will multiply them for your glory, in the name of Jesus Christ. (Luke 16:10)
10. O Lord, I thank you for opening doors of opportunity and bringing increase into my life. (Isaiah 45:2)
11. I declare that my faith in you will move mountains and break every financial limitation in my life, in the name of Jesus Christ. (Mark 11:23)
12. Heavenly Father, I release a spirit of generosity and giving in my life, knowing that as I give, it will be given back to me in abundance. (Luke 6:38)
13. I declare that every seed I sow into your kingdom will produce a harvest of blessings and increase, in the name of Jesus Christ. (2 Corinthians 9:6)
14. Almighty Lord, I rebuke the devourer that has come against my finances, and I declare restoration and multiplication, in the name of Jesus Christ. (Malachi 3:11)
15. I declare that my financial struggles are temporary, and I will walk in permanent breakthrough and prosperity, in the name of Jesus Christ. (Psalm 30:5)
16. O God my Father, I declare that you are my shepherd, and I shall not want. you lead me beside still waters and restore my soul. (Psalm 23:1-3)
17. I declare that I have the power to create wealth, as you have given me the ability to succeed, in the name of Jesus Christ. (Deuteronomy 8:18)
18. Lord, I thank you for giving me ideas, strategies, and favor to excel in my career and business endeavors. (Proverbs 16:3)
19. I declare that I am a lender and not a borrower, and I will walk in financial independence. (Deuteronomy 28:12)

20. Heavenly Father, I surrender my finances to you and ask for your divine guidance in managing them wisely. (Proverbs 3:5-6)
21. I declare that every financial setback will be turned into a comeback, and I will experience miraculous restoration, in the name of Jesus Christ. (Joel 2:25)
22. Lord, I thank you for giving me the ability to produce wealth, that your covenant may be established on the earth. (Deuteronomy 8:18)
23. I declare that doors of opportunity and provision are opening for me, and I will walk through them in faith, in the name of Jesus Christ. (Revelation 3:8)
24. O Lord my Father, I rebuke the spirit of lack and poverty, and I declare a season of abundance and increase in my life, in the name of Jesus Christ. (Psalm 35:27)
25. I declare that my financial struggles are not a reflection of my worth, but I am fearfully and wonderfully made by you. (Psalm 139:14)
26. Lord, I thank you for blessing the work of my hands and causing me to prosper in all that I do. (Psalm 90:17)
27. I declare that I am an heir of God and a joint heir with Christ, and I will experience the inheritance of abundance, in the name of Jesus Christ. (Romans 8:17)
28. Heavenly Father, I surrender all my financial worries to you and trust that you will provide all my needs according to your riches. (Philippians 4:6-7)
29. I declare that I am a money magnet, and I attract wealth, opportunities, and divine connections into my life. (Proverbs 10:22)
30. Lord, I thank you for giving me the ability to create multiple streams of income and to be a blessing to others. (Ecclesiastes 11:1)

31. I declare that I am breaking free from the cycle of financial struggle and entering into a season of financial breakthrough. (Isaiah 61:7)
32. O Lord my Father, I declare that my financial future is secure in your hands, and you will lead me into prosperity. (Jeremiah 29:11)
33. I declare that I am a tither, and as I honor you with my finances, you will pour out blessings I cannot contain, in the name of Jesus Christ. (Malachi 3:10)
34. My Father and my Lord, I thank you for giving me the power to overcome any financial challenge that comes my way. (1 John 4:4)
35. I declare that my income will exceed my expenses, and I will have an abundance to bless others. (2 Corinthians 9:8)
36. Heavenly Father, I repent for any wrong financial decisions I have made, and I ask for your forgiveness and restoration. (Joel 2:25-26)
37. I declare that I have the mind of Christ, and I will make wise financial choices that align with your will. (1 Corinthians 2:16)
38. My Lord, I thank you for breaking every cycle of poverty and lack in my family lineage, and I will walk in generational blessings, in the name of Jesus Christ. (Galatians 3:13-14)
39. I declare that I am a conduit of financial blessings, and as I give, I will receive multiplied blessings in return. (Luke 6:38)
40. Father, I declare that my faith is activating supernatural provision and abundance in my life. (Hebrews 11:6)
41. I declare that my financial struggles are being turned into testimonies of your faithfulness and provision. (Psalm 40:2)
42. Lord, I thank you for blessing me to be a blessing to others, and I will use my finances to advance your kingdom. (Proverbs 11:24-25)

43. I declare that my trust is in you alone, and I will not be moved by financial challenges or circumstances. (Psalm 125:1)
44. I declare that I have an abundance mindset, and I will not be limited by scarcity or fear, in the name of Jesus Christ. (2 Corinthians 9:8)
45. Heavenly Father, I surrender my financial struggles to you and trust that you will turn them into opportunities for growth and increase, in the name of Jesus Christ. (Romans 8:28)
46. I declare that I am sowing seeds of faith and obedience, and I will reap a harvest of blessings and provision. (Galatians 6:7)
47. Lord, I thank you for opening doors of divine connections and partnerships that will lead to financial breakthroughs. (Proverbs 18:16)
48. I declare that my financial breakthrough is imminent, and I will experience a season of supernatural increase. (Isaiah 60:22)
49. Father, I declare that my financial struggles do not define me, but your promises and plans for my life do. (Jeremiah 29:11)
50. I declare that I am an overcomer in every area of my life, including my finances, and I will walk in victory, in the name of Jesus Christ. (1 John 5:4)

DAY 8

Breaking the Cycle of Repeated Failures: Experiencing Victory and Success

We all face challenges and setbacks in life, but it can be disheartening when these failures seem to repeat themselves. Breaking free from the cycle of repeated failures requires a shift in mindset and a renewed perspective. By drawing strength from the wisdom found in scripture, we can find inspiration, guidance, and the faith to overcome obstacles and experience victory and success.

- Embrace God's Promises:
  Scripture offers a wealth of promises from God that assure us of His faithfulness and desire for our well-being. Jeremiah 29:11 states, *"For I know the plans I have for you, declares the LORD, plans to prosper you and not to harm you, plans to give you hope and a future."* Meditate on these promises, internalize them, and let them fuel your perseverance during times of failure.

- Seek God's Wisdom:
  Proverbs 3:5-6 advises, *"Trust in the LORD with all your heart and lean not on your own understanding; in all your ways submit to him, and he will make your paths straight."* When we face failures, it's crucial to turn to God for wisdom and guidance. By seeking His direction, we can break free from the patterns that lead to repeated failures and discover new strategies for success.

- Learn from Past Mistakes:
  Failure is an opportunity for growth and learning. Proverbs 24:16 reminds us, *"For though the righteous fall seven times, they rise again."* Instead of dwelling on past failures, take time to reflect on the lessons they hold. Analyze your mistakes, identify patterns, and make necessary adjustments to your approach. With each failure, you become wiser, stronger, and better equipped for future success.

- Develop Resilience:
  Resilience is the ability to bounce back from setbacks and keep moving forward. In James 1:2-4, we are encouraged to *"Consider it pure joy, my brothers and sisters, whenever you face trials of many kinds because you know that the testing of your faith produces perseverance."* Embrace challenges as opportunities for growth and allow them to refine your character. Cultivate a resilient spirit that refuses to be defined by failures but rather rises above them.

- Walk by Faith, not by Sight:
  2 Corinthians 5:7 reminds us to *"walk by faith, not by sight."* It's easy to become discouraged when we see failures, but faith calls us to look beyond the present circumstances. Trust in God's plan and timing, even when it seems like success is elusive. By aligning our perspective with God's promises, we can move forward with confidence and experience victory, regardless of past failures.

Breaking the cycle of repeated failures requires a steadfast belief in God's promises, a humble seeking of His wisdom, and a determination to learn from past mistakes. By embracing resilience and walking by faith, we can overcome obstacles and achieve the success we desire. Remember, failure is not the end but a steppingstone towards greater accomplishments. With God's guidance and the transformative power of scripture, we can break free from the cycle of repeated failures and experience true victory and success.

Confession & Declaration:

In the name of Jesus, I declare that the powers of darkness operating against me are broken! According to Ephesians 6:12, *"For we do not wrestle against flesh and blood, but against the rulers, against the authorities, against the cosmic powers over this present darkness, against the spiritual forces of evil in the heavenly places."* I stand firm in the authority I have in Christ, and I rebuke every demonic force that seeks to hinder my progress and well-being.

I declare that I am a child of God, redeemed by the blood of Jesus. Romans 8:37 declares, *"No, in all these things we are more than conquerors through him who loved us."* I reject any power of darkness that tries to intimidate or oppress me, for I am more than a conqueror through Christ!

I declare that I am filled with the Holy Spirit and His power resides within me. 2 Timothy 1:7 assures me that *"God gave us a spirit not of fear but of power and love and self-control."* I reject fear and any stronghold of darkness, knowing that I have the power to overcome through the Spirit of God.

I declare that every curse spoken against me is nullified by the power of the cross. Galatians 3:13 says, *"Christ redeemed us from the curse of the law by becoming a curse for us."* I proclaim my freedom from every generational curse, every spoken curse, and every witchcraft attack. I am washed clean by the blood of Jesus.

I declare that I walk in the light of God's truth, and the lies of darkness have no power over me. Psalm 27:1 affirms, *"The Lord is my light and my salvation; whom shall I fear?"* I reject every lie, deception, and manipulation of the enemy. I stand on the truth of God's Word and declare victory over the powers of darkness.

I stand firm in these declarations, knowing that God's Word is powerful and cannot be broken, and that God is faithful to bring deliverance and victory in every area of my life. I trust in His promises and rest in His unfailing love.

Prayer of Deliverance

1. Heavenly Father, I declare that I am breaking the cycle of repeated failures in my life. (Philippians 4:13)
2. Lord, I thank you for granting me the power to overcome every obstacle and experience victory and success. (Romans 8:37)
3. I declare that failure is not my portion, and I am destined for success in all areas of my life, in the name of Jesus Christ. (Jeremiah 29:11)
4. Lord, I release any negative patterns or cycles that have held me back, and I step into a season of breakthrough and triumph. (Isaiah 43:18-19)
5. I declare that my past failures do not define me, and I am moving forward into a future filled with achievements and accomplishments, in the name of Jesus Christ. (2 Corinthians 5:17)
6. Heavenly Father, I break every generational curse of failure and declare a new legacy of success and prosperity in my family, in the name of Jesus Christ. (Deuteronomy 30:19)
7. I renounce the spirit of failure and embrace the spirit of excellence and victory in all that I do, in the name of Jesus Christ. (Daniel 6:3)

8. Lord, I declare that I am an overcomer, and I have the strength to conquer every challenge that comes my way. (1 John 5:4)
9. I reject the fear of failure and embrace the courage to take risks and step out in faith towards my dreams and goals. (Joshua 1:9)
10. I declare that I am not a victim of circumstances but a victor through Christ who strengthens me. (Philippians 4:13)
11. Heavenly Father, I thank you for your promise to bless the work of my hands and make me successful in all that I do. (Deuteronomy 28:12)
12. I declare that I am a vessel of honor and purpose, and my life is filled with divine opportunities for success. (2 Timothy 2:21)
13. Lord, I break free from the bondage of past failures and mistakes, and I embrace a future filled with triumph and victory. (Psalm 34:17)
14. I declare that I am not limited by my past failures, but I am empowered by the grace of God to achieve greatness. (Ephesians 2:8-9)
15. Heavenly Father, I release forgiveness towards myself for past failures and mistakes and receive your mercy and grace to move forward. (Psalm 103:12)
16. I declare that I am surrounded by a divine favor that opens doors of success and opportunities beyond my imagination. (Psalm 5:12)
17. Lord, I reject the spirit of defeat and embrace the spirit of perseverance and resilience to overcome every setback. (Romans 12:12)
18. I declare that my mind is renewed, and I am filled with positive thoughts and beliefs that lead me to success. (Romans 12:2)
19. Heavenly Father, I surrender my plans and ambitions to you and trust in your divine guidance to lead me to success. (Proverbs 3:5-6)
20. I declare that failure is not the end but a steppingstone towards greater achievements and breakthroughs. (Proverbs 24:16)

21. Lord, I break free from the chains of self-doubt and insecurity and walk in confidence, knowing that I am capable of success. (Philippians 1:6)
22. I declare that setbacks and failures do not define my worth, for I am fearfully and wonderfully made by God. (Psalm 139:14)
23. Heavenly Father, I thank you for equipping me with the skills and talents necessary to excel in every area of my life. (1 Peter 4:10)
24. I declare that I am anointed for success, and every project or endeavor I undertake prospers in your hands. (Psalm 1:3)
25. Lord, I surrender my fear of failure and embrace a mindset of courage and boldness to pursue my dreams. (Isaiah 41:10)
26. I declare that I am a conqueror, and nothing can separate me from the love and provision of God. (Romans 8:38-39)
27. Heavenly Father, I break every negative word spoken over my life and replace it with your promises of success and victory. (Isaiah 54:17)
28. I declare that failure is an opportunity for growth and learning, and I will use it as a steppingstone to greater achievements. (James 1:2-4)
29. Lord, I declare that I am diligent and committed to my goals, and I will not be swayed by distractions or discouragement. (Proverbs 21:5)
30. I declare that success and prosperity follow me wherever I go, for I am a child of the Most High God. (Deuteronomy 28:8)
31. Heavenly Father, I break every stronghold of failure in my life and declare your victory and favor over every area. (2 Corinthians 10:4)
32. I declare that I am not limited by my past mistakes but empowered by your grace to rise above them and achieve success. (2 Corinthians 12:9)

33. Lord, I declare that my thoughts and words align with your promises of success, and I speak life and blessings into my future. (Proverbs 18:21)
34. I declare that failure is not the end of my story but a steppingstone towards a greater purpose and destiny. (Romans 8:28)
35. Heavenly Father, I thank you for surrounding me with wise counsel and mentors who guide me towards success. (Proverbs 13:20)
36. I declare that I am resilient and persistent, and I will keep pressing forward until I achieve the success I desire. (Galatians 6:9)
37. Lord, I release any self-sabotaging behaviors and habits that hinder my progress towards success and embrace self-discipline and focus. (1 Corinthians 9:24-27)
38. I declare that my faith in God's promises sustains me through every trial and leads me to victory and success. (Hebrews 11:1)
39. Heavenly Father, I surrender my disappointments and failures to you and receive your peace and restoration in return. (Psalm 51:12)
40. I declare that I am a vessel of divine ideas and creativity, and I will use them to achieve success and make a positive impact. (Ephesians 2:10)
41. Lord, I declare that I am more than a conqueror through Christ Jesus who loves me and empowers me to succeed. (Romans 8:37)
42. I declare that failure has no power over me, for God's grace and favor go before me and make a way for success. (Psalm 84:11)
43. I reject the spirit of complacency and embrace a spirit of excellence and continuous improvement in all that I do. (Colossians 3:23)

44. Heavenly Father, I thank you for the gifts and talents you have bestowed upon me, and I will use them to bring glory to your name through my success. (1 Peter 4:10-11)
45. I declare that I am not defined by my past failures, but I am defined by the righteousness of Christ and his victory over sin and death, in the name of Jesus Christ. (2 Corinthians 5:21)
46. Lord, I break free from the bondage of comparison and competition and focus on running my own race towards success. (Hebrews 12:1)
47. I declare that I am led by the Holy Spirit, and he guides me towards success and prosperity in all my endeavors. (Galatians 5:25)
48. Heavenly Father, I release any feelings of unworthiness or inadequacy and embrace my identity as a child of God, destined for greatness and success. (1 John 3:1)
49. I declare that my failures do not define me, but my resilience and determination to keep going in the face of adversity lead me to success. (Proverbs 24:16)
50. Lord, I declare that I am walking in alignment with your will for my life, and as I trust in you, I will experience victory and success beyond measure, in the name of Jesus Christ. (Psalm 37:5)

DAY 9

Breaking the Spirit of Rejection: Request God's Healing and Deliverance

Have you ever felt like an outsider? Have you experienced the pain of rejection, where you constantly question your worth and struggle to form healthy relationships? If so, you may be battling with the spirit of rejection. This insidious force can influence our thoughts, emotions, and actions, leading us down a path of self-destructive patterns. But there is hope! By seeking God's healing and deliverance, we can break free from the clutches of rejection and experience the abundant life He has promised us.

The spirit of rejection thrives on our vulnerabilities and past hurts. It whispers lies into our ears, convincing us that we are unwanted, unlovable, and unworthy. These lies can manifest in various aspects of our lives, from personal relationships to professional endeavors. However, as children of God, we have the power to overcome this spirit and find true freedom.

The first step towards breaking the spirit of rejection is acknowledging its existence. We must recognize the negative patterns it has instilled in our lives and the influence it has had on our relationships. Once we acknowledge the problem, we can bring it before God in prayer, asking Him for healing and deliverance. Psalm 34:17-18 reminds us that *"The righteous cry out, and the LORD hears them; he delivers them from all their troubles. The LORD is close to the brokenhearted and saves those who are crushed in spirit."* God is ready and willing to listen to our cries for help and rescue us from the grip of rejection.

In our journey towards healing, it is crucial to immerse ourselves in God's Word. The Bible is filled with stories of individuals who faced rejection but found solace and restoration in the arms of their Heavenly Father. One such example is found in Isaiah 41:10, where God reassures us, saying, *"So do not fear, for I am with you; do not be dismayed, for I am your God. I will strengthen you and help you; I will uphold you with my righteous right hand."* By meditating on these promises, we can find comfort and strength in the midst of our struggles.

Furthermore, we must surrender our hurts and insecurities to God. The spirit of rejection often feeds on our unresolved pain, using it as fuel to keep us in bondage. However, when we surrender our brokenness to God, He can begin the process of healing and restoration. Jeremiah 29:11 declares, *"For I know the plans I have for you,"* declares the LORD, *"plans to prosper you and not to harm you, plans to give you hope and a future."* Trusting in God's plans for our lives allows us to release the burden of rejection and embrace the hope He has promised.

Additionally, seeking support from a trusted community can be instrumental in breaking free from the spirit of rejection. God often works through the love and encouragement of others to bring healing and restoration to our lives. Galatians 6:2 urges us to *"Carry each other's burdens, and in this way, you will fulfill the law of Christ."* Connecting with fellow believers who can provide guidance, prayer, and accountability can help us navigate the journey towards wholeness.

Finally, it is essential to remember that our identity is rooted in Christ, not in the opinions or actions of others. Ephesians 1:4-5 assures us that *"For he chose us in him before the creation of the world to be holy and blameless in his sight. In love, he predestined us for adoption to sonship through Jesus Christ, in accordance with his pleasure and will."* Regardless of the rejection we may have faced, we are chosen and loved by God. Embracing this truth enables us to rise above the lies of rejection and walk confidently in our identity as children of the Most High.

Breaking the spirit of rejection is a journey that requires perseverance, faith, and a deep reliance on God's healing power. As we surrender our pain, immerse ourselves in His Word, seek support from a community, and embrace our identity in Christ, we can experience the freedom and abundant life God has prepared for us. Let us boldly request God's healing and deliverance, confident that He is faithful to answer our prayers and lead us towards wholeness.

Confession & Declaration:

In the name of Jesus, I declare that the powers of darkness operating against me are broken! According to Ephesians 6:12, *"For we do not wrestle against flesh and blood, but against the rulers, against the authorities, against the cosmic powers over this present darkness, against the spiritual forces of evil in the heavenly places."* I stand firm in the authority I have in Christ, and I rebuke every demonic force that seeks to hinder my progress and well-being.

I declare that I am a child of God, redeemed by the blood of Jesus. Romans 8:37 declares, *"No, in all these things we are more than conquerors through him who loved us."* I reject any power of darkness that tries to intimidate or oppress me, for I am more than a conqueror through Christ!

I declare that I am filled with the Holy Spirit and His power resides within me. 2 Timothy 1:7 assures me that *"God gave us a spirit not of fear but of power and love and self-control."* I reject fear and any stronghold of darkness, knowing that I have the power to overcome through the Spirit of God.

I declare that every curse spoken against me is nullified by the power of the cross. Galatians 3:13 says, *"Christ redeemed us from the curse of the law by becoming a curse for us."* I proclaim my freedom from every generational curse, every spoken curse, and every witchcraft attack. I am washed clean by the blood of Jesus.

I declare that I walk in the light of God's truth, and the lies of darkness have no power over me. Psalm 27:1 affirms, *"The Lord is my light and my salvation; whom shall I fear?"* I reject every lie, deception, and manipulation of the enemy. I stand on the truth of God's Word and declare victory over the powers of darkness.

I stand firm in these declarations, knowing that God's Word is powerful and cannot be broken, and that God is faithful to bring deliverance and victory in every area of my life. I trust in His promises and rest in His unfailing love.

Prayer of Deliverance

1. Heavenly Father, I come before you today, asking for your healing touch upon my wounded heart. I declare that the spirit of rejection has no power over me, for I am accepted and loved by you. (Ephesians 1:6)
2. Lord, I renounce and reject every lie that the spirit of rejection has spoken over my life. I declare that I am fearfully and wonderfully made in your image. (Psalm 139:14)
3. I declare that I am chosen by you, Lord, a royal priesthood, a holy nation. I am set apart for your divine purposes, and rejection has no place in my life. (1 Peter 2:9)
4. Father, I thank you for your unconditional love. I declare that your love casts out all fear, including the fear of rejection. (1 John 4:18)

5. Lord, I surrender all the pain of rejection to you. I declare that you are my refuge and strength, a present help in times of trouble. (Psalm 46:1)
6. I declare that I am deeply loved and accepted by you, O Lord. Your love surrounds me and fills every void of rejection within me. (Romans 8:38-39)
7. Heavenly Father, I reject the spirit of rejection and embrace the spirit of adoption. I declare that I am your beloved child, chosen and cherished. (Romans 8:15)
8. I declare that I am forgiven and redeemed through the blood of Jesus Christ. Rejection has no power over me because I am accepted by you, Lord. (Ephesians 1:7)
9. Lord, I declare that I am complete in you. I am lacking nothing, for you meet all my needs according to your riches in glory. (Colossians 2:10, Philippians 4:19)
10. I renounce the lies of rejection and declare the truth of your Word over my life. I am fearfully and wonderfully made, and I am loved beyond measure, in the name of Jesus Christ. (Psalm 139:14)
11. Father, I declare that I am more than a conqueror through Christ Jesus. The spirit of rejection cannot prevail against me, for I am victorious in Him. (Romans 8:37)
12. I declare that I have the mind of Christ. I am filled with His love, joy, and peace, and rejection has no power to steal my peace and confidence in Him, in the name of Jesus Christ. (1 Corinthians 2:16)
13. Lord, I choose to forgive those who have rejected me. I release them into your hands and ask for your healing in my heart. (Matthew 6:14-15)
14. I declare that your perfect love casts out all fear, including the fear of rejection. Your love surrounds me and empowers me to walk in freedom and confidence. (1 John 4:18)

15. Father, I declare that I am accepted into your family. I am a joint heir with Christ and share in His inheritance. Rejection has no authority over my identity in you. (Romans 8:17)
16. I renounce the spirit of self-rejection and declare that I am fearfully and wonderfully made by your hand, Lord. I embrace my unique identity and purpose in you. (Psalm 139:14)
17. I declare that I am an overcomer through Christ who strengthens me. The spirit of rejection cannot define me or hinder me from fulfilling your plans for my life, in the name of Jesus Christ. (Philippians 4:13)
18. Lord, I choose to place my identity in you alone. I reject the approval of man and seek only your approval, for you are the One who truly matters. (Galatians 1:10)
19. I declare that I am an ambassador for Christ, chosen and appointed by Him. Rejection has no power over my calling and purpose in spreading His love and truth. (2 Corinthians 5:20)
20. Heavenly Father, I declare that I am rooted and grounded in your love. I am established in your truth, and rejection cannot uproot me from the firm foundation I have in you, in the name of Jesus Christ. (Ephesians 3:17)
21. I declare that I am a vessel of honor, sanctified and useful to you, Lord. I reject the lies of rejection and embrace the truth of my worth and significance in you. (2 Timothy 2:21)
22. Lord, I declare that I am more than enough in you. Your grace is sufficient for me, and I find my identity and worth in you alone. (2 Corinthians 12:9)
23. I reject the spirit of comparison and declare that I am uniquely created and called by you, Lord. I will not measure my worth based on the opinions of others. (Galatians 6:4)
24. Father, I declare that I am blessed and highly favored by you. Rejection has no power to diminish the blessings you have in store for me. (Ephesians 1:3)

25. I declare that I am accepted into the beloved, chosen by you before the foundation of the world. Your acceptance defines my identity, not the opinions of others. (Ephesians 1:6)
26. Lord, I declare that your plans for me are good and not for harm, to give me a future and a hope. Rejection cannot alter the destiny you have ordained for me, in the name of Jesus Christ. (Jeremiah 29:11)
27. I declare that I am clothed with garments of salvation and covered with the robe of righteousness. Rejection cannot strip away the righteousness I have in Christ, in the name of Jesus Christ. (Isaiah 61:10)
28. Heavenly Father, I declare that I am a temple of the Holy Spirit. Rejection has no place within me, for your Spirit dwells within me, filling me with your love and acceptance. (1 Corinthians 6:19)
29. I renounce the spirit of fear and declare that I have been given a spirit of power, love, and a sound mind. Rejection cannot control or intimidate me, in the name of Jesus Christ. (2 Timothy 1:7)
30. I declare that I am set free from the bondage of rejection. Your truth has set me free, and I will walk in the freedom and victory you have provided. (John 8:32)
31. Lord, I declare that you are my shepherd, and I shall not want. You lead me beside still waters and restore my soul. Rejection has no power to steal my peace and rest in you. (Psalm 23:1-3)
32. I declare that I am an overcomer by the blood of the Lamb and the word of my testimony. The spirit of rejection cannot silence my voice or rob me of my victory, in the name of Jesus Christ. (Revelation 12:11)
33. I declare that I am rooted in the love of Christ. I am firmly planted in His grace and mercy, and rejection cannot uproot me from His unchanging love. (Ephesians 3:17-18)

34. Father, I declare that I am a masterpiece created in Christ Jesus for good works. Rejection cannot diminish the value and purpose you have bestowed upon me. (Ephesians 2:10)
35. I declare that I am an overcomer through Him who loves me. The spirit of rejection has no power over me because I am covered by your unfailing love. (Romans 8:37-39)
36. I declare that I am blessed with every spiritual blessing in heavenly places in Christ. Rejection cannot steal the abundant blessings you have poured out upon me. (Ephesians 1:3)
37. Lord, I declare that your perfect love casts out all fear, including the fear of rejection. I will not be bound by fear, for your love empowers and protects me. (1 John 4:18)
38. I renounce the lies of rejection and declare the truth that I am chosen and loved by you. I am a precious child of God, and rejection has no place in my identity. (1 Peter 2:9)
39. I declare that I am fearfully and wonderfully made. Your hand has crafted every part of me, and I am accepted and loved by you, O Lord. (Psalm 139:14)
40. Lord, I declare that you are my stronghold and my deliverer. You are my shield, and rejection cannot penetrate your divine protection over my life, in the name of Jesus Christ. (Psalm 18:2)
41. I declare that I am a vessel of honor, sanctified and set apart for your glory. Rejection cannot define me, for I am chosen and approved by you. (2 Timothy 2:21)
42. Heavenly Father, I declare that I am complete in you. In your presence, there is fullness of joy, and rejection cannot steal the joy and completeness I find in you. (Colossians 2:10)
43. I declare that I am an heir of God and a joint heir with Christ. Rejection cannot diminish my inheritance and the abundant blessings you have prepared for me. (Romans 8:17)

44. I renounce the spirit of self-rejection and declare that I am fearfully and wonderfully made by your hand, Lord. I embrace my unique identity and purpose in you. (Psalm 139:14)
45. I declare that I am deeply loved by you, O Lord. Your love covers me, surrounds me, and fills every void of rejection within me, in the name of Jesus Christ. (Romans 8:38-39)
46. Lord, I choose to forgive those who have rejected me. I release them into your hands and ask for your healing in my heart, in the name of Jesus Christ. (Matthew 6:14-15)
47. I declare that I am accepted and cherished by you, my heavenly Father. Your love for me is unfailing and everlasting, and rejection cannot alter your love for me. (Jeremiah 31:3)
48. I declare that I am fearfully and wonderfully made in your image, Lord. Rejection has no power to distort or diminish the beauty and worth you have bestowed upon me. (Genesis 1:27)
49. I renounce the spirit of comparison and declare that I am uniquely created and called by you. I will not measure my worth based on the opinions of others. (Galatians 6:4)
50. Father, I declare that your plans for me are good and not for harm. I trust in your faithfulness and love, knowing that you will bring healing and deliverance from the spirit of rejection, in the name of Jesus Christ. (Jeremiah 29:11)

DAY 10

Breaking Patterns of Sickness and Disease: Experiencing Divine Health and Wholeness

In a world where sickness and disease seem to be pervasive, it is essential to discover the truth about divine health and wholeness. Many individuals find themselves trapped in a cycle of ill health, unaware of the power they possess to break free from this pattern. By understanding the promises of divine healing found within sacred scriptures, we can embark on a transformative journey towards experiencing a life of vitality, strength, and well-being.

- Recognizing the Divine Blueprint for Health:
  The Bible is replete with verses that reveal God's desire for His children to live in health and wholeness. In Exodus 15:26, the Lord declares, *"I am the Lord, your healer,"* demonstrating His intention to heal and restore. Additionally, in 3 John 1:2, we are reminded that it is God's will for us to prosper and be in good health, even as our soul prospers. Understanding that divine health is part of God's design empowers us to break free from the patterns of sickness and disease.

- Embracing the Power of Faith:
  Faith plays a crucial role in experiencing divine health and wholeness. Jesus often emphasized the connection between faith and healing during His earthly ministry. In Matthew 9:22, He tells a woman who had been suffering from bleeding, *"Your faith has made you well."* Similarly, in Mark 11:24, Jesus teaches that when we pray, we should believe that we have

received what we ask for, and it will be granted. Cultivating a strong faith in God's healing power enables us to break the cycle of sickness and disease.

- Activating the Healing Power of God's Word:
  Scripture is a powerful tool for overcoming sickness and disease. In Proverbs 4:20-22, we are encouraged to pay attention to God's words, for they are life and health to our bodies. By meditating on healing scriptures, such as Psalm 103:2-3, which declares, *"Praise the Lord, my soul, and forget not all his benefits— who forgives all your sins and heals all your diseases,"* we can tap into the divine healing power of God's Word and break free from the patterns of ill health.

- Partnering with God through Prayer and Thankfulness:
  Prayer is a direct line of communication with our Heavenly Father, enabling us to seek His healing touch. In James 5:16, we are encouraged to pray for one another, acknowledging that the prayer of a righteous person is powerful and effective. By bringing our physical ailments before God in prayer and expressing gratitude for His healing provision, we align ourselves with His divine plan for our health and wholeness.

Breaking free from the patterns of sickness and disease requires a shift in mindset and a deepening of our relationship with God. By recognizing His desire for our health and well-being, embracing the power of faith, activating the healing power of God's Word, and partnering with Him through prayer and thankfulness, we can experience divine health and wholeness. As we delve into the scriptures, we discover a loving and compassionate God who invites us to live a life of vitality and freedom from the bondage of ill health. May we all embark on this transformative journey towards experiencing the fullness of divine health that God intends for us.

Confession & Declaration:

In the name of Jesus, I declare that the powers of darkness operating against me are broken! According to Ephesians 6:12, *"For we do not wrestle against flesh and blood, but against the rulers, against the authorities, against the cosmic powers over this present darkness, against the spiritual forces of evil in the heavenly places."* I stand firm in the authority I have in Christ, and I rebuke every demonic force that seeks to hinder my progress and well-being.

I declare that I am a child of God, redeemed by the blood of Jesus. Romans 8:37 declares, *"No, in all these things we are more than conquerors through him who loved us."* I reject any power of darkness that tries to intimidate or oppress me, for I am more than a conqueror through Christ!

I declare that I am filled with the Holy Spirit and His power resides within me. 2 Timothy 1:7 assures me that *"God gave us a spirit not of fear but of power and love and self-control."* I reject fear and any stronghold of darkness, knowing that I have the power to overcome through the Spirit of God.

I declare that every curse spoken against me is nullified by the power of the cross. Galatians 3:13 says, *"Christ redeemed us from the curse of the law by becoming a curse for us."* I proclaim my freedom from every generational curse, every spoken curse, and every witchcraft attack. I am washed clean by the blood of Jesus.

I declare that I walk in the light of God's truth, and the lies of darkness have no power over me. Psalm 27:1 affirms, *"The Lord is my light and my salvation; whom shall I fear?"* I reject every lie, deception, and manipulation of the enemy. I stand on the truth of God's Word and declare victory over the powers of darkness.

I stand firm in these declarations, knowing that God's Word is powerful and cannot be broken, and that God is faithful to bring deliverance and victory in every area of my life. I trust in His promises and rest in His unfailing love.

Prayer of Deliverance

1. Heavenly Father, I declare that sickness and disease have no power over me, for you are my healer. (Exodus 15:26)
2. I break every generational pattern of sickness and disease in my family, in the name of Jesus. (Exodus 20:5)
3. By the stripes of Jesus, I declare that I am healed and made whole, in the name of Jesus Christ. (Isaiah 53:5)
4. I renounce any agreement I have made with sickness and disease and declare my allegiance to divine health. (James 4:7)
5. I command every sickness and disease in my body to bow down to the name of Jesus and leave, never to return. (Philippians 2:9-10)
6. I declare that my body is the temple of the Holy Spirit, and no sickness or disease has a place in it. (1 Corinthians 6:19-20)
7. I break the power of any curse or witchcraft sent against my health and declare divine protection over my body, in the name of Jesus Christ. (Psalm 91:3)
8. I reject fear and anxiety concerning my health, for God has not given me a spirit of fear but of power, love, and a sound mind. (2 Timothy 1:7)
9. I declare that the Word of God is health to my flesh, and it brings life to every cell in my body. (Proverbs 4:22)

10. I release the healing power of God's Word into every organ, tissue, and system of my body, bringing divine health and wholeness, in the name of Jesus Christ. (Psalm 107:20)
11. I declare that my immune system is strong and fortified, protecting me from every form of sickness and disease, in the name of Jesus Christ. (Isaiah 41:10)
12. I break the power of any genetic predisposition to sickness and disease and declare divine DNA alignment in my body, in the name of Jesus Christ. (Psalm 139:14)
13. I reject any diagnosis that contradicts the truth of God's Word and declare that I am fearfully and wonderfully made. (Psalm 139:14)
14. I release the healing power of forgiveness in my life, letting go of bitterness and resentment that can hinder my health. (Matthew 6:14-15)
15. I declare that divine health is my inheritance as a child of God, and I receive it by faith. (Psalm 103:2-3)
16. I renounce any unhealthy habits or lifestyle choices that have contributed to sickness and disease in my body, in the name of Jesus Christ. (1 Corinthians 6:19-20)
17. I speak life and health over every cell, tissue, and organ in my body, declaring that they function in perfect harmony. (Proverbs 18:21)
18. I release the power of God's love to heal any emotional wounds that have manifested as physical ailments in my body, in the name of Jesus Christ. (Psalm 147:3)
19. I declare that divine health and wholeness flow through my bloodstream, cleansing and restoring every part of my body. (Mark 5:34)
20. I reject the spirit of infirmity and declare that I walk in divine strength and vitality, in the name of Jesus Christ. (Luke 13:12-13)

21. I release the power of God's peace into my mind and body, knowing that peace brings healing and restoration. (Philippians 4:7)
22. I declare that my body is a temple of the Holy Spirit, and I honor God by taking care of it through proper nutrition and exercise. (1 Corinthians 6:19-20)
23. I break the power of any word curse spoken against my health and declare that the words of my mouth align with God's promises of healing. (Proverbs 18:21)
24. I declare that every cell, tissue, and organ in my body aligns with the perfect health blueprint of heaven. (Jeremiah 30:17)
25. I command every sickness and disease to dry up at the root and be cast into the sea, never to return, in the name of Jesus Christ. (Mark 11:23)
26. I release the healing power of God's Word into every cell of my body, transforming it into a vessel of divine health, in the name of Jesus Christ. (Romans 12:2)
27. I reject the spirit of death and declare that I will live and not die, declaring the works of the Lord, in the name of Jesus Christ. (Psalm 118:17)
28. I declare that divine health and wholeness are my portion, and I walk in the fullness of God's healing power, in the name of Jesus Christ. (3 John 1:2)
29. I renounce any agreement I have made with fear and doubt concerning my health and declare my faith in God's healing promises. (Mark 5:36)
30. I release the power of God's joy into my life, knowing that a joyful heart is good medicine for my body. (Proverbs 17:22)
31. I declare that my body is not subject to the limitations of this world but is transformed by the power of God's Spirit. (Romans 8:11)

32. I break the power of any soul ties or ungodly connections that have contributed to sickness and disease in my body, in the name of Jesus Christ. (1 Corinthians 6:15-17)
33. I release the healing power of God's love into every area of my life, bringing restoration and wholeness. (1 Peter 4:8)
34. I declare that my body is a temple of the Holy Spirit, and I yield to the Spirit's guidance for my health and well-being. (1 Corinthians 3:16)
35. I break the power of any negative words spoken over my health and declare that God's promises of healing are my reality, in the name of Jesus Christ. (Proverbs 12:18)
36. I declare that my body is fearfully and wonderfully made, and I celebrate the intricate design and functionality of every part. (Psalm 139:14)
37. I release the power of God's peace into any areas of stress or anxiety in my life, knowing that peace brings healing. (Isaiah 26:3)
38. I reject any thoughts or beliefs that undermine my faith in God's healing power and declare that I am fully persuaded of His promises. (Romans 4:20-21)
39. I declare that my body is a vessel of divine health, radiating God's glory and goodness to the world around me, in the name of Jesus Christ. (Matthew 5:16)
40. I release the power of God's Word to uproot and destroy any hidden causes of sickness and disease in my body, in the name of Jesus Christ. (Hebrews 4:12)
41. I declare that God's supernatural healing power flows through me, restoring and renewing every part of my being, in the name of Jesus Christ. (Psalm 103:3)
42. I break the power of any negative emotions or toxic thought patterns that have contributed to sickness and disease in my body. (2 Corinthians 10:5)

43. I declare that I am an overcomer, and no weapon formed against my health shall prosper. (Isaiah 54:17)
44. I release the power of God's grace into my life, knowing that His grace is sufficient for my healing and restoration. (2 Corinthians 12:9)
45. I renounce any agreement I have made with the spirit of infirmity and declare that I am free and victorious in Christ. (Galatians 5:1)
46. I declare that divine health is my birthright as a child of God, and I walk in the authority and power given to me. (Luke 10:19)
47. I release the healing power of God's Spirit into every cell, tissue, and organ in my body, bringing alignment and renewal, in the name of Jesus Christ. (Romans 8:2)
48. I declare that I am surrounded by the healing presence of God, and His love and mercy encompass me. (Psalm 32:10)
49. I break the power of any unbelief or doubt concerning my healing and declare my unwavering faith in God's promises, in the name of Jesus Christ. (Mark 9:23)
50. I declare that I am an agent of divine health and healing, and I release God's healing power to touch and transform lives around me. (Matthew 10:8)

DAY 11

Breaking the Cycle of Negative Words: A Journey of Transformation

Words have incredible power. They can build up, inspire, and encourage, but they can also tear down, discourage, and hinder our growth. Negative words spoken over our lives can create a cycle of self-doubt, limiting beliefs, and a distorted self-image. However, as we turn to the Scriptures, we find powerful promises and truths that can help us break free from the cycle of negative words and experience transformation in our lives.

- Embracing God's Truth:
  Proverbs 18:21 says, *"Death and life are in the power of the tongue."* We must recognize that the negative words spoken over us do not align with God's truth. Instead, we need to fill our minds with His promises. Philippians 4:8 encourages us to dwell on whatever is true, honorable, just, pure, lovely, and commendable.

- Overcoming Limiting Beliefs:
  Negative words can shape our beliefs about ourselves and our abilities. Yet, God's Word declares that we are fearfully and wonderfully made (Psalm 139:14) and that we can do all things through Christ who strengthens us (Philippians 4:13). By renewing our minds with these truths, we can break free from limiting beliefs and embrace our full potential.

- Speaking Life:

In order to break the cycle of negative words, we must replace them with words of life. Proverbs 15:4 says, *"A gentle tongue is a tree of life, but perverseness in it breaks the spirit."* Let our words be filled with kindness, encouragement, and affirmation, both towards ourselves and others. When we speak life, we create an atmosphere of positivity and empowerment.

- Surrounding Ourselves with Encouragement:
  Negative words can have a lasting impact on our mindset, but surrounding ourselves with positive influences can counteract their effects. Proverbs 27:17 reminds us that *"iron sharpens iron,"* emphasizing the importance of cultivating relationships with people who speak life, encouragement, and truth into our lives. Choose friends, mentors, and communities that build you up.

- Finding Identity in Christ:
  Ultimately, our true identity is found in Christ, not in the negative words spoken over us. 2 Corinthians 5:17 tells us, *"Therefore, if anyone is in Christ, he is a new creation. The old has passed away; behold, the new has come."* When we anchor our identity in Christ, we can find healing, restoration, and a renewed sense of purpose.

Breaking the cycle of negative words is a journey that requires intentionality, faith, and perseverance. As we immerse ourselves in God's truth, renew our minds, speak life, surround ourselves with encouragement, and find our identity in Christ, we can experience a transformative power that breaks the chains of negativity and propels us into a life filled with purpose and joy.

Remember, you are loved, valued, and destined for greatness. Let God's words shape your life, and watch as the cycle of negativity is shattered, paving the way for a future filled with hope and abundant blessings.

Confession & Declaration:

In the name of Jesus, I declare that the powers of darkness operating against me are broken! According to Ephesians 6:12, *"For we do not wrestle against flesh and blood, but against the rulers, against the authorities, against the cosmic powers over this present darkness, against the spiritual forces of evil in the heavenly places."* I stand firm in the authority I have in Christ, and I rebuke every demonic force that seeks to hinder my progress and well-being.

I declare that I am a child of God, redeemed by the blood of Jesus. Romans 8:37 declares, *"No, in all these things we are more than conquerors through him who loved us."* I reject any power of darkness that tries to intimidate or oppress me, for I am more than a conqueror through Christ!

I declare that I am filled with the Holy Spirit and His power resides within me. 2 Timothy 1:7 assures me that *"God gave us a spirit not of fear but of power and love and self-control."* I reject fear and any stronghold of darkness, knowing that I have the power to overcome through the Spirit of God.

I declare that every curse spoken against me is nullified by the power of the cross. Galatians 3:13 says, *"Christ redeemed us from the curse of the law by becoming a curse for us."* I proclaim my freedom from every generational curse, every spoken curse, and every witchcraft attack. I am washed clean by the blood of Jesus.

I declare that I walk in the light of God's truth, and the lies of darkness have no power over me. Psalm 27:1 affirms, *"The Lord is my light and my salvation; whom shall I fear?"* I reject every lie, deception, and manipulation of the enemy. I stand on the truth of God's Word and declare victory over the powers of darkness.

I stand firm in these declarations, knowing that God's Word is powerful and cannot be broken, and that God is faithful to bring deliverance and victory in every area of my life. I trust in His promises and rest in His unfailing love.

Prayer of Deliverance

1. Heavenly Father, I thank you for your Word, which is truth and life. I declare that every negative word spoken over my life is nullified by the power of your truth, in the name of Jesus Christ. (Proverbs 18:21)
2. Lord, I repent for any agreement I have made with negative words spoken over me. I break every soul tie formed through those words and declare my identity in Christ. (Galatians 2:20)
3. I renounce every curse and negative declaration spoken over my life, for I am a child of God, redeemed by the blood of Jesus. (Galatians 3:13)
4. I command every negative word spoken against me to be uprooted and cast into the sea, in the name of Jesus Christ. I choose to receive only words of blessing and life. (Matthew 21:21)
5. In the name of Jesus, I break the power of every negative word spoken by others or myself. I declare that I am fearfully and wonderfully made, and I walk in the destiny God has prepared for me. (Psalm 139:14)
6. Heavenly Father, let the power of your Holy Spirit cleanse my mind from every negative thought and word spoken over me.

Help me to focus on what is true, noble, and praiseworthy, in the name of Jesus Christ. (Philippians 4:8)
7. I declare that I have the mind of Christ, and I am transformed by the renewing of my mind. I reject negative thoughts and words and embrace your promises and truth, in the name of Jesus Christ. (Romans 12:2)
8. Lord, I break every word curse that has been passed down through generations in my family. I declare that I am a new creation in Christ Jesus. (2 Corinthians 5:17)
9. I release forgiveness to those who have spoken negative words over me. I choose not to hold any grudges or bitterness, but to walk in love and forgiveness. (Ephesians 4:32)
10. I declare that I am an overcomer through Christ Jesus. No weapon formed against me shall prosper, and every tongue that rises against me in judgment shall be condemned, in the name of Jesus Christ. (Isaiah 54:17)
11. Heavenly Father, I ask for your protection over my ears and heart. Help me to guard what I listen to and receive, so that only words of life and encouragement enter my spirit, in the name of Jesus Christ. (Proverbs 4:23)
12. I declare that my words align with your Word, O Lord. I speak life, blessings, and encouragement to myself and others. May my words be a source of healing and hope, in the name of Jesus Christ. (Proverbs 16:24)
13. I rebuke every negative word that has caused fear, doubt, and insecurity in my life. I declare that I am rooted and grounded in God's love, and His perfect love casts out all fear. (1 John 4:18)
14. Lord, I surrender every negative word spoken over my health. I declare that by Jesus' stripes, I am healed. I receive your divine health and restoration in my body, in the name of Jesus Christ. (Isaiah 53:5)
15. I renounce every negative word that has been spoken over my finances. I declare that God is my provider, and I walk in His

abundance and prosperity, in the name of Jesus Christ. (Philippians 4:19)
16. I reject every negative word that has caused relational strain and brokenness. I declare that I walk in love, forgiveness, and reconciliation. My relationships are blessed and restored, in the name of Jesus Christ. (Colossians 3:13)
17. Heavenly Father, I break the power of every negative word that has hindered my spiritual growth. I declare that I am growing in grace and the knowledge of Jesus Christ. (2 Peter 3:18)
18. I declare that I am anointed and appointed for a purpose. Every negative word spoken against my calling is canceled, and I walk confidently in the destiny God has for me, in the name of Jesus Christ. (1 John 2:27)
19. Lord, I break the power of negative words that have caused me to feel unworthy or insignificant, in the name of Jesus Christ. I declare that I am chosen, accepted, and dearly loved by God. (1 Peter 2:9)
20. I renounce every negative word spoken over my mind and emotions. I declare that I have the peace of God that surpasses all understanding, guarding my heart and mind in Christ Jesus. (Philippians 4:7)
21. I command every negative word spoken over my children and family to be nullified. I declare that my children are blessed, protected, and walking in the fear of the Lord, in the name of Jesus Christ. (Psalm 112:2)
22. Heavenly Father, I break the power of every negative word spoken by spiritual authorities. I declare that your Word and truth prevail over any false pronouncements or curses, in the name of Jesus Christ. (Matthew 16:19)
23. I reject every negative word that has caused me to doubt my abilities and talents. I declare that I am uniquely gifted by God, and I use my talents for His glory. (1 Peter 4:10)

24. I break the power of every negative word spoken over my dreams and aspirations. I declare that God's plans for me are good, and He brings them to fruition, in the name of Jesus Christ. (Jeremiah 29:11)
25. Lord, I break every negative word that has created a spirit of defeat and discouragement within me. I declare that I am more than a conqueror through Him who loved me. (Romans 8:37)
26. I renounce every negative word spoken over my spiritual authority. I declare that I honor and submit to godly leadership, knowing that obedience brings blessings. (Hebrews 13:17)
27. I reject every negative word spoken over my past mistakes and failures. I declare that I am forgiven, washed clean by the blood of Jesus, and I walk in His righteousness. (1 John 1:9)
28. Heavenly Father, grant me wisdom and discernment to recognize and reject every negative word spoken by the enemy. I choose to stand firm on your promises and resist the lies of the devil, in the name of Jesus Christ. (James 4:7)
29. I declare that no negative word spoken against me shall prosper. I am like a tree planted by rivers of water, bearing fruit in every season, and whatever I do shall prosper. (Psalm 1:3)
30. I renounce every negative word that has caused me to question my worth and value. I declare that I am a precious jewel in God's sight, and He delights in me. (Isaiah 62:3)
31. I break the power of every negative word spoken over my marriage. I declare that my marriage is blessed, strong, and filled with love, unity, and harmony, in the name of Jesus Christ. (Ephesians 5:33)
32. Lord, grant me your grace and strength to guard my tongue and speak words of life, encouragement, and edification. May my words build up and bring hope to others, in the name of Jesus Christ. (Ephesians 4:29)

33. I reject every negative word spoken over my future. I declare that my future is bright and filled with God's purpose and provision, in the name of Jesus Christ. (Jeremiah 29:11)
34. I renounce every negative word spoken over my self-image and body. I declare that I am fearfully and wonderfully made, created in the image of God. (Psalm 139:14)
35. I break the power of every negative word spoken over my abilities and skills. I declare that I can do all things through Christ who strengthens me. (Philippians 4:13)
36. I declare that I am an overcomer of negative words and their effects. I am rooted in the truth of God's Word, and His Word empowers me to walk in victory. (1 John 5:4)
37. I renounce every negative word spoken over my purpose and calling. I declare that I am an instrument of God's Kingdom, making a significant impact for His glory. (2 Timothy 1:9)
38. O Lord my Father, let the power of your Holy Spirit fill my mouth with words of wisdom, grace, and truth. May my words bring life and blessing to those around me, in the name of Jesus Christ. (Colossians 4:6)
39. I break the power of every negative word spoken over my education and intellectual capacity. I declare that I have the mind of Christ and receive wisdom and understanding from Him, in the name of Jesus Christ. (1 Corinthians 2:16)
40. I declare that I am surrounded by a shield of divine protection. No negative word or harm shall come near me or my loved ones, in the name of Jesus Christ. (Psalm 91:11)
41. I renounce every negative word spoken over my potential and possibilities. I declare that with God, all things are possible, and I can do exceedingly, abundantly above all I ask or think. (Ephesians 3:20)
42. I break the power of every negative word spoken over my emotions and mental well-being. I declare that I have the peace of God that guards my heart and mind. (Philippians 4:7)

43. I declare that I am an ambassador for Christ, carrying His light and love wherever I go. Every negative word spoken against my testimony is silenced, and lives are transformed through me, in the name of Jesus Christ. (2 Corinthians 5:20)
44. Lord, I surrender every negative word spoken over my dreams and visions. I declare that your promises for my life are yes and amen. I walk in faith, knowing that you are faithful. (2 Corinthians 1:20)
45. I renounce every negative word spoken over my friendships and relationships. I declare that I attract godly connections and walk in love, unity, and mutual edification, in the name of Jesus Christ. (Proverbs 27:17)
46. I declare that I am filled with the fruit of the Spirit. Every negative word spoken against my character is nullified, and I walk in love, joy, peace, patience, kindness, goodness, faithfulness, gentleness, and self-control. (Galatians 5:22-23)
47. I break the power of every negative word spoken over my potential for success and prosperity. I declare that I am blessed to be a blessing, and I walk in the overflow of God's provision, in the name of Jesus Christ. (Deuteronomy 28:8)
48. I renounce every negative word spoken over my spiritual giftings and ministries. I declare that I operate in the power of the Holy Spirit, and my giftings bring glory to God and benefit to others, in the name of Jesus Christ. (1 Peter 4:10)
49. I declare that I am a vessel of honor, sanctified and useful for the master's work. Every negative word spoken against my purpose is rendered powerless, and I walk in divine assignments, in the name of Jesus Christ. (2 Timothy 2:21)
50. Heavenly Father, I thank you for your faithfulness and for the power of your Word. I choose to align my words and thoughts with your truth. I declare victory over every negative word spoken over my life, in Jesus' name. Amen. (John 8:32)

DAY 12

Breaking the Cycle of Ancestral Loneliness: Embracing Genuine Relationships

Loneliness can be a pervasive and deeply distressing emotion, affecting individuals across generations. Sometimes, it seems as though this feeling has been passed down through the ages, creating a cycle of ancestral loneliness. However, as we delve into the realm of genuine relationships, we can find solace and break free from this cycle. Let us explore the importance of authentic connections and discover how scripture can guide us on this transformative journey.

- Recognizing the Desire for Connection
  In the book of Genesis, we read that it is not good for humans to be alone (Genesis 2:18). God designed us to be relational beings, craving connection and companionship. Acknowledging this innate longing within ourselves is the first step in breaking the cycle of ancestral loneliness. We must embrace the truth that we were made for community.

- Prioritizing Authenticity over Superficiality
  In today's fast-paced and digital world, it is easy to settle for superficial relationships. However, true fulfillment comes from genuine connections. Proverbs 27:17 reminds us that iron sharpens iron, indicating that deep bonds are formed through meaningful interactions. Instead of seeking shallow connections, let us invest time and effort into building authentic relationships that nurture our souls.

- Extending Love and Kindness
  To break the cycle of loneliness, we must extend love and kindness to others. The commandment to love our neighbors as ourselves (Mark 12:31) emphasizes the importance of treating others with compassion and empathy. By showing genuine care and concern, we can foster meaningful connections and inspire others to do the same.

- Cultivating a Supportive Community
  Hebrews 10:24-25 encourages us to consider how we may spur one another on toward love and good deeds, while also emphasizing the significance of gathering together. Surrounding ourselves with a supportive community helps us combat loneliness. Engaging in activities with like-minded individuals and sharing our joys and struggles creates a sense of belonging that can break the ancestral cycle of loneliness.

- Seeking Divine Connection
  While human relationships are vital, we should not neglect our connection with the divine. Psalm 16:11 states, *"You make known to me the path of life; you will fill me with joy in your presence."* Recognizing that God is always with us can provide solace in times of loneliness. Through prayer, meditation, and studying scripture, we can develop a deep spiritual relationship that transcends human limitations.

Breaking the cycle of ancestral loneliness requires intentionality and a genuine desire to foster meaningful connections. By recognizing our innate longing for connection, prioritizing authenticity, extending love and kindness, cultivating a supportive community, and seeking divine connection, we can embark on a transformative journey toward breaking free from the chains of loneliness.

Remember, breaking the cycle of ancestral loneliness is not an overnight process. It requires consistent effort, vulnerability, and a willingness to step out of our comfort zones. However, as we embrace genuine relationships and align ourselves with the wisdom found in scripture, we can find healing, fulfillment, and ultimately, break the chains of ancestral loneliness once and for all.

Confession & Declaration:

In the name of Jesus, I declare that the powers of darkness operating against me are broken! According to Ephesians 6:12, *"For we do not wrestle against flesh and blood, but against the rulers, against the authorities, against the cosmic powers over this present darkness, against the spiritual forces of evil in the heavenly places."* I stand firm in the authority I have in Christ, and I rebuke every demonic force that seeks to hinder my progress and well-being.

I declare that I am a child of God, redeemed by the blood of Jesus. Romans 8:37 declares, *"No, in all these things we are more than conquerors through him who loved us."* I reject any power of darkness that tries to intimidate or oppress me, for I am more than a conqueror through Christ!

I declare that I am filled with the Holy Spirit and His power resides within me. 2 Timothy 1:7 assures me that *"God gave us a spirit not of fear but of power and love and self-control."* I reject fear and any stronghold of darkness, knowing that I have the power to overcome through the Spirit of God.

I declare that every curse spoken against me is nullified by the power of the cross. Galatians 3:13 says, *"Christ redeemed us from the curse of the law by becoming a curse for us."* I proclaim my freedom from every generational curse, every spoken curse, and every witchcraft attack. I am washed clean by the blood of Jesus.

I declare that I walk in the light of God's truth, and the lies of darkness have no power over me. Psalm 27:1 affirms, *"The Lord is my light and my salvation; whom shall I fear?"* I reject every lie, deception, and manipulation of the enemy. I stand on the truth of God's Word and declare victory over the powers of darkness.

I stand firm in these declarations, knowing that God's Word is powerful and cannot be broken, and that God is faithful to bring deliverance and victory in every area of my life. I trust in His promises and rest in His unfailing love.

Prayer of Deliverance

1. Heavenly Father, I declare that I break the ancestral cycle of loneliness in my life and embrace genuine relationships. Psalm 68:6
2. I renounce every spirit of isolation and declare that I am surrounded by a community of loving and supportive people. Ecclesiastes 4:9-10
3. I reject the lie of being alone and declare that God is always with me, and He will never leave me nor forsake me. Hebrews 13:5
4. I break every generational curse of loneliness that has plagued my family line and declare freedom in Christ. Galatians 3:13-14
5. I declare that I am fearfully and wonderfully made, and I deserve to experience healthy and fulfilling relationships. Psalm 139:14
6. I release forgiveness towards those who have caused me pain and choose to walk in love and reconciliation. Ephesians 4:32

7. I renounce the spirit of rejection and declare that I am accepted and beloved by God and His people. Ephesians 1:6
8. I break every unhealthy pattern of isolation and declare a season of divine connections and meaningful relationships. Proverbs 18:24
9. I declare that I attract genuine friendships that align with God's purpose for my life. Proverbs 27:17
10. I break every soul tie with unhealthy relationships and declare emotional healing and restoration. Isaiah 61:1-3
11. I reject the spirit of self-pity and declare that God's love and grace empower me to overcome loneliness. 2 Corinthians 12:9
12. I declare that my loneliness is replaced with God's peace and joy that surpasses all understanding. Philippians 4:7
13. I renounce every lie that I am unworthy of love and declare that God's love for me is unconditional. Romans 8:38-39
14. I break every curse of abandonment and declare that God's faithfulness surrounds me always. Deuteronomy 31:6
15. I declare that I am a magnet for healthy, loving, and lasting relationships that bring glory to God. Proverbs 17:17
16. I reject the spirit of fear that hinders me from forming deep connections, and I embrace God's perfect love that casts out fear. 1 John 4:18
17. I renounce every negative mindset that keeps me isolated, and I declare a renewed mind that embraces God's truth about community. Romans 12:2
18. I declare that I am a blessing to others and a source of encouragement and support in their lives. 1 Thessalonians 5:11
19. I break every cycle of emotional detachment and declare a season of vulnerability and authentic connections. Romans 12:15
20. I renounce the spirit of loneliness that leads to despair and declare that God's presence brings hope and purpose to my life. Jeremiah 29:11

21. I declare that I am not alone, for the Holy Spirit dwells within me and guides me into meaningful relationships. John 14:16-18
22. I break every bondage of past hurts and declare that I am free to love and be loved without fear. 1 John 4:7-8
23. I renounce every spirit of self-isolation and declare that I am called to be part of a vibrant community of believers. Hebrews 10:24-25
24. I declare that I have the power to break free from the cycle of loneliness through Christ who strengthens me. Philippians 4:13
25. I reject the lie that my worth is defined by my relationship status and declare that my value is found in being a child of God. 1 John 3:1
26. I renounce every lie that tells me I am unlovable and declare that I am deeply loved and cherished by God. Zephaniah 3:17
27. I break every chain of isolation and declare that I am connected to a network of believers who uplift and encourage one another. Romans 12:5
28. I declare that God's grace empowers me to extend forgiveness and build bridges of reconciliation in my relationships. Colossians 3:13
29. I renounce the spirit of withdrawal and declare that I am an active participant in nurturing and cultivating meaningful connections. Proverbs 27:9
30. I declare that I am a magnet for healthy and godly friendships that align with my purpose and destiny. Proverbs 13:20
31. I break every generational pattern of relational dysfunction and declare that I am walking in God's design for healthy relationships. Genesis 2:18
32. I renounce every spirit of self-reliance and declare my dependence on God and His people for love, support, and companionship. Ecclesiastes 4:12

33. I declare that I am an agent of love and unity, and I actively pursue reconciliation and harmony in my relationships. 1 Peter 3:8
34. I reject the lie that I am too damaged to experience healthy relationships and declare that God's healing power restores me for meaningful connections. Psalm 147:3
35. I declare that I am a carrier of God's love, and wherever I go, I bring comfort, encouragement, and joy to those around me. 2 Corinthians 1:3-4
36. I renounce the spirit of comparison that breeds discontentment and declare that I am content in Christ and appreciative of the relationships I have. Philippians 4:11
37. I break every curse of betrayal and declare that I am surrounded by trustworthy friends who honor and respect me. Proverbs 17:17
38. I declare that God is opening doors for me to connect with like-minded individuals who share my values and passions. 1 Corinthians 1:10
39. I renounce every spirit of isolation and declare that I am positioned for divine appointments and encounters that lead to deep relationships. Acts 2:42-47
40. I declare that I am a peacemaker and a bridge-builder, fostering unity and harmony among the people around me. Matthew 5:9
41. I break every bondage of fear that hinders me from reaching out and forming new connections, and I embrace God's courage to step into new relationships. Joshua 1:9
42. I renounce the spirit of unworthiness that keeps me from pursuing meaningful relationships and declare that I am chosen and called by God. 1 Peter 2:9
43. I declare that I am a vessel of God's love, and I extend compassion and kindness to others, cultivating deep and lasting connections. Colossians 3:12

44. I reject every lie that tells me I am destined to be alone, and I declare that God's plan for me includes fulfilling relationships. Psalm 68:6
45. I declare that I am never alone, for God's presence surrounds me, and His love envelops me at all times. Psalm 139:7-10
46. I renounce every spirit of pride that isolates me from others, and I humbly embrace the beauty of community and shared experiences. James 4:6
47. I break every stronghold of loneliness and declare that God's perfect love fills every void in my heart, bringing wholeness and restoration. 1 John 4:16
48. I declare that I am a conduit of God's grace, extending forgiveness and second chances to those who have hurt me. Ephesians 4:32
49. I renounce the lies that I am unlovable and unwanted, and I declare that God's love for me is deep, unconditional, and everlasting. Jeremiah 31:3
50. I declare that I am breaking free from the chains of ancestral loneliness, and I am stepping into a season of vibrant and authentic relationships, bringing glory to God's name. Romans 12:16

DAY 13

Breaking the Cycle of Self-Sabotage: Embracing Unhindered Progress and Success

Have you ever found yourself on the brink of achieving success, only to witness your own self-sabotaging behaviors holding you back? Many of us have experienced this cycle at some point in our lives. Self-sabotage can manifest in various ways, such as negative self-talk, fear of failure, procrastination, or even self-destructive habits. However, as believers, we have access to timeless wisdom that can help us break free from this detrimental pattern. Today, we will explore how embracing unhindered progress and success is possible by believing the truth of the Word of God.

- Overcoming Negative Self-Talk:
  One of the most common ways we sabotage ourselves is through negative self-talk. We tend to doubt our abilities, belittle our achievements, and constantly compare ourselves to others. However, the Scriptures remind us of our inherent worth and the power of positive thinking. Philippians 4:13 declares, *"I can do all things through Christ who strengthens me."* By anchoring our thoughts in this truth and replacing self-doubt with affirmations of faith, we can break free from the cycle of self-sabotage.

- Conquering the Fear of Failure:
  Fear of failure often paralyzes us, preventing us from taking risks and seizing opportunities. But God's Word assures us that He is with us every step of the way. Joshua 1:9 encourages us,

"Have I not commanded you? Be strong and courageous. Do not be afraid; do not be discouraged, for the Lord your God will be with you wherever you go." By placing our trust in God and acknowledging that failure is a part of growth, we can overcome the fear that hinders our progress and experience true success.

- Defeating Procrastination:
  Procrastination is a common form of self-sabotage that robs us of our time and potential. However, the Bible provides us with wisdom on how to combat this habit. Proverbs 13:4 reminds us, *"The soul of the sluggard craves and gets nothing, while the soul of the diligent is richly supplied."* By cultivating discipline, setting achievable goals, and relying on the Holy Spirit for guidance and strength, we can overcome procrastination and make consistent progress towards our goals.

- Breaking Free from Self-Destructive Habits:
  Self-destructive habits, whether they involve unhealthy relationships, addictions, or negative coping mechanisms, can hinder our progress and success. However, the Scriptures offer hope for transformation and deliverance. Romans 12:2 encourages us, *"Do not conform to the pattern of this world but be transformed by the renewing of your mind."* Through prayer, seeking professional help if needed, and relying on God's grace, we can break free from self-destructive patterns and embrace a life of freedom and success.

Breaking the cycle of self-sabotage is an essential step towards embracing unhindered progress and success. By anchoring ourselves in the timeless wisdom of the Scriptures, we can overcome negative self-talk, conquer the fear of failure, defeat procrastination, and break free from self-destructive habits. As we align our thoughts and actions with

God's promises, we can experience the abundant life He has planned for us. Remember, with God's guidance and our willingness to embrace positive change, we can break free from self-sabotage and embrace the success and progress we were destined for.

Confession & Declaration:

In the name of Jesus, I declare that the powers of darkness operating against me are broken! According to Ephesians 6:12, *"For we do not wrestle against flesh and blood, but against the rulers, against the authorities, against the cosmic powers over this present darkness, against the spiritual forces of evil in the heavenly places."* I stand firm in the authority I have in Christ, and I rebuke every demonic force that seeks to hinder my progress and well-being.

I declare that I am a child of God, redeemed by the blood of Jesus. Romans 8:37 declares, *"No, in all these things we are more than conquerors through him who loved us."* I reject any power of darkness that tries to intimidate or oppress me, for I am more than a conqueror through Christ!

I declare that I am filled with the Holy Spirit and His power resides within me. 2 Timothy 1:7 assures me that *"God gave us a spirit not of fear but of power and love and self-control."* I reject fear and any stronghold of darkness, knowing that I have the power to overcome through the Spirit of God.

I declare that every curse spoken against me is nullified by the power of the cross. Galatians 3:13 says, *"Christ redeemed us from the curse of the law by becoming a curse for us."* I proclaim my freedom from every generational curse, every spoken curse, and every witchcraft attack. I am washed clean by the blood of Jesus.

I declare that I walk in the light of God's truth, and the lies of darkness have no power over me. Psalm 27:1 affirms, *"The Lord is my light and my salvation; whom shall I fear?"* I reject every lie, deception, and manipulation of the enemy. I stand on the truth of God's Word and declare victory over the powers of darkness.

I stand firm in these declarations, knowing that God's Word is powerful and cannot be broken, and that God is faithful to bring deliverance and victory in every area of my life. I trust in His promises and rest in His unfailing love.

Prayer of Deliverance

1. Heavenly Father, I declare that I am breaking the cycle of self-sabotage in my life. Your Word says in Philippians 4:13, *"I can do all things through Christ who strengthens me."*
2. Lord, I renounce every negative thought and limiting belief that has held me back. I embrace the truth that I am fearfully and wonderfully made according to Psalm 139:14.
3. I declare that I am releasing the past and moving forward into a season of unhindered progress and success. Isaiah 43:18-19 reminds me, *"Forget the former things; do not dwell on the past. See, I am doing a new thing!"*
4. Heavenly Father, I break every chain of self-doubt and insecurity that has hindered my progress. Your Word assures me in 2 Timothy 1:7 that, *"God has not given us a spirit of fear, but of power and of love and of a sound mind."*
5. I declare that I am no longer a slave to procrastination and laziness. I am disciplined and focused, knowing that *"Whatever you do, work at it with all your heart, as working for the Lord"* (Colossians 3:23).

6. Lord, I reject the spirit of self-sabotage and embrace the spirit of excellence. I choose to do everything with excellence for your glory, according to Daniel 6:3, in the name of Jesus Christ.
7. I declare that I am breaking free from the cycle of self-destructive habits. Your Word says in Romans 12:2, *"Do not conform to the pattern of this world but be transformed by the renewing of your mind."*
8. Heavenly Father, I release forgiveness towards myself for past mistakes and failures. Your Word promises in 1 John 1:9 that, *"If we confess our sins, he is faithful and just and will forgive us our sins and purify us from all unrighteousness."*
9. I declare that I am embracing a mindset of abundance and prosperity. I believe in the truth of Deuteronomy 8:18, *"But remember the Lord your God, for it is he who gives you the ability to produce wealth."*
10. Lord, I renounce every negative word spoken over my life and declare that I am walking in the fullness of my purpose. Psalm 139:16 assures me that, *"Your eyes saw my unformed body; all the days ordained for me were written in your book before one of them came to be."*
11. I declare that I am breaking free from the fear of failure. I trust in the promise of Joshua 1:9, *"Be strong and courageous. Do not be afraid; do not be discouraged, for the Lord your God will be with you wherever you go."*
12. Heavenly Father, I surrender my self-sabotaging behaviors to you. Help me to walk in obedience to your Word and experience the abundant life you have planned for me, as stated in John 10:10.
13. I declare that I am no longer a victim of circumstances but a victor in Christ. Romans 8:37 assures me that, *"In all these things, we are more than conquerors through him who loved us."*

14. Lord, I break the power of negative patterns and generational curses over my life, in the name of Jesus Christ. Your Word promises in Galatians 3:13-14, *"Christ redeemed us from the curse of the law by becoming a curse for us."*
15. I declare that I am breaking free from comparison and embracing my unique journey. Psalm 139:16 reminds me that, *"Your eyes saw my unformed body; all the days ordained for me were written in your book before one of them came to be."*
16. Heavenly Father, I reject the lies of the enemy that say I am not worthy of success. I embrace the truth that I am a child of God and co-heir with Christ, according to Romans 8:17, in the name of Jesus Christ.
17. I declare that I am renewing my mind daily with your Word. I am transforming my thinking to align with your truth, as instructed in Romans 12:2.
18. Lord, I rebuke every spirit of self-sabotage that has hindered my progress. Your Word assures me in James 4:7, *"Submit yourselves, then, to God. Resist the devil, and he will flee from you."*
19. I declare that I am stepping out of my comfort zone and taking risks for the sake of my destiny. I trust in the promise of Isaiah 41:10, *"So do not fear, for I am with you; do not be dismayed, for I am your God."*
20. Heavenly Father, I surrender my need for control and trust in your divine guidance. Proverbs 3:5-6 encourages me to, *"Trust in the LORD with all your heart and lean not on your own understanding."*
21. I declare that I am breaking free from the bondage of past failures. Your Word assures me in Philippians 3:13-14 that, *"Forgetting what is behind and straining toward what is ahead, I press on toward the goal to win the prize for which God has called me heavenward in Christ Jesus."*

22. Lord, I reject the spirit of self-criticism and embrace self-compassion. I choose to see myself through your eyes, as a beloved child of God, according to 1 John 3:1.
23. I declare that I am embracing a mindset of gratitude and thanksgiving. I choose to focus on the goodness of God and His faithfulness, as instructed in 1 Thessalonians 5:18.
24. Heavenly Father, I break every curse of self-sabotage spoken over my life. I declare the truth of Isaiah 54:17, *"No weapon forged against you will prevail."*
25. I declare that I am walking in divine favor and open doors of opportunity. Your Word promises in Psalm 84:11, *"For the LORD God is a sun and shield; the LORD bestows favor and honor; no good thing does he withhold from those whose walk is blameless."*
26. Lord, I renounce the spirit of perfectionism and embrace progress over perfection. I trust in your ability to use my imperfections for your glory, as stated in 2 Corinthians 12:9.
27. I declare that I am breaking free from the bondage of people-pleasing. I seek to please God above all else, knowing that *"Am I now trying to win the approval of human beings, or of God? Or am I trying to please people? If I were still trying to please people, I would not be a servant of Christ"* (Galatians 1:10).
28. Heavenly Father, I reject every negative label that has been placed upon me. I embrace my identity as your child, chosen and loved, as declared in 1 Peter 2:9.
29. I declare that I am no longer controlled by my past mistakes. I am forgiven and redeemed by the blood of Jesus Christ, as affirmed in Ephesians 1:7.
30. Lord, I break the power of self-sabotaging habits and addictions in my life. Your Word assures me in 2 Corinthians 5:17 that, *"Therefore, if anyone is in Christ, the new creation has come: The old has gone, the new is here!"*

31. I declare that I am stepping into a season of divine acceleration. Your Word promises in Isaiah 60:22, *"I am the LORD; in its time I will do this swiftly."*
32. Heavenly Father, I release the need to compare myself with others. I embrace the truth that you have a unique plan and purpose for my life, as affirmed in Jeremiah 29:11.
33. I declare that I am breaking free from the stronghold of negative self-talk. I choose to speak life and affirmations over myself, according to Proverbs 18:21.
34. Lord, I surrender my fears and insecurities to you. I trust in your strength and guidance, knowing that *"The LORD is my light and my salvation—whom shall I fear? The LORD is the stronghold of my life—of whom shall I be afraid?"* (Psalm 27:1).
35. I declare that I am embracing a lifestyle of self-care and self-love. I recognize that my body is a temple of the Holy Spirit, as stated in 1 Corinthians 6:19-20.
36. Heavenly Father, I break the power of negative influences and toxic relationships in my life. Your Word assures me in Proverbs 13:20, *"Walk with the wise and become wise, for a companion of fools suffers harm."*
37. I declare that I am breaking free from the bondage of financial lack and poverty mindset. I trust in your provision and believe in the truth of Philippians 4:19, *"And my God will meet all your needs according to the riches of his glory in Christ Jesus."*
38. Lord, I renounce every self-imposed limitation and embrace the truth that I can do all things through Christ. Philippians 4:13 reminds me, *"I can do all this through him who gives me strength."*
39. I declare that I am breaking free from the stronghold of fear of rejection. I trust in your acceptance and love for me, as affirmed in Romans 8:38-39.

40. Heavenly Father, I release the need for external validation and embrace my identity in Christ. Your Word assures me in 1 Peter 2:9 that, *"But you are a chosen people, a royal priesthood, a holy nation, God's special possession."*
41. I declare that I am breaking free from the cycle of self-sabotage in my relationships. I choose to walk in love, forgiveness, and grace, as instructed in Ephesians 4:32.
42. Lord, I surrender my need for control and trust in your perfect timing. Your Word promises in Ecclesiastes 3:11, *"He has made everything beautiful in its time."*
43. I declare that I am breaking free from the bondage of self-pity and embracing a mindset of gratitude. Your Word encourages me in 1 Thessalonians 5:16-18, *"Rejoice always, pray continually, give thanks in all circumstances; for this is God's will for you in Christ Jesus."*
44. Heavenly Father, I break every curse of self-sabotage and declare blessings over my life. Your Word promises in Deuteronomy 28:13, *"The LORD will make you the head, not the tail. If you pay attention to the commands of the LORD your God that I give you this day and carefully follow them, you will always be at the top, never at the bottom."*
45. I declare that I am breaking free from the bondage of perfectionism and embracing progress. I trust in your ability to use my imperfect efforts for your glory, as stated in Philippians 1:6.
46. Lord, I renounce every negative thought pattern and embrace the truth of your Word. I choose to meditate on what is true, noble, right, pure, lovely, admirable, excellent, and praiseworthy, as encouraged in Philippians 4:8.
47. I declare that I am breaking free from the spirit of self-sabotage in my career. I am walking in alignment with your purpose for my life, as stated in Proverbs 16:3, *"Commit to the LORD whatever you do, and he will establish your plans."*

48. Heavenly Father, I release every mindset of scarcity and embrace the abundance of your blessings. Your Word assures me in Psalm 23:5, *"You prepare a table before me in the presence of my enemies. you anoint my head with oil; my cup overflows."*
49. I declare that I am breaking free from the cycle of negative self-talk. I choose to speak life, encouragement, and affirmation over myself, according to Ephesians 4:29.
50. Lord, I surrender my desires and dreams to you. I trust in your perfect plan for my life and believe that you are able to do immeasurably more than all I ask or imagine, according to Ephesians 3:20.

DAY 14

Breaking the Cycle of Fear of Failure: Stepping into New Opportunities with Courage and Confidence

Fear of failure can often hold us back from pursuing new opportunities and reaching our full potential. The fear of not succeeding or making mistakes can become a paralyzing force, preventing us from taking the necessary steps towards growth and success. However, as believers, we have access to a powerful source of courage and confidence that can help us break free from this cycle of fear. By embracing the wisdom found in Scripture, we can overcome our fear of failure and step into new opportunities with courage and confidence.

- Embrace God's Promises:
  In the face of fear, it is essential to hold onto the promises of God. Joshua 1:9 reminds us, *"Have I not commanded you? Be strong and courageous. Do not be frightened, and do not be dismayed, for the Lord your God is with you wherever you go."* This verse reassures us that God is always with us, providing strength and courage in times of uncertainty. By meditating on God's promises, we can find the confidence to step into new opportunities.

- Shift Your Perspective:
  Often, our fear of failure stems from a skewed perspective on success. Instead of viewing failure as something to be feared, we can choose to see it as an opportunity for growth. Proverbs 24:16 encourages us, *"For the righteous falls seven times and*

rises again." This verse reminds us that even the most righteous individuals experience setbacks, but they do not let failure define them. Embracing a growth mindset allows us to learn from our mistakes and approach new opportunities with a renewed sense of confidence.

- Trust in God's Guidance:
  When stepping into new opportunities, it is crucial to trust in God's guidance rather than relying solely on our own understanding. Proverbs 3:5-6 advises, *"Trust in the Lord with all your heart, and do not lean on your own understanding. In all your ways acknowledge him, and he will make straight your paths."* By seeking God's wisdom and following His lead, we can overcome the fear of failure and trust that He will guide us on the right path.

- Surround Yourself with Encouragement:
  Surrounding ourselves with a supportive community of believers can play a significant role in overcoming the fear of failure. Hebrews 10:24-25 encourages us to *"consider how to stir up one another to love and good works, not neglecting to meet together."* Being part of a community that uplifts and encourages us helps build our confidence and reminds us that we are not alone in our journey. Together, we can face new opportunities with courage, knowing that we have a network of support.

Breaking the cycle of fear of failure is a journey that requires courage, faith, and reliance on God. By embracing God's promises, shifting our perspective, trusting in His guidance, and surrounding ourselves with a supportive community, we can step into new opportunities with confidence. Let us remember the words of Philippians 4:13, *"I can do all things through him who strengthens me."* With God's strength, we can conquer our fears and embrace the abundant life He has planned for us.

Confession & Declaration:

In the name of Jesus, I declare that the powers of darkness operating against me are broken! According to Ephesians 6:12, *"For we do not wrestle against flesh and blood, but against the rulers, against the authorities, against the cosmic powers over this present darkness, against the spiritual forces of evil in the heavenly places."* I stand firm in the authority I have in Christ, and I rebuke every demonic force that seeks to hinder my progress and well-being.

I declare that I am a child of God, redeemed by the blood of Jesus. Romans 8:37 declares, *"No, in all these things we are more than conquerors through him who loved us."* I reject any power of darkness that tries to intimidate or oppress me, for I am more than a conqueror through Christ!

I declare that I am filled with the Holy Spirit and His power resides within me. 2 Timothy 1:7 assures me that *"God gave us a spirit not of fear but of power and love and self-control."* I reject fear and any stronghold of darkness, knowing that I have the power to overcome through the Spirit of God.

I declare that every curse spoken against me is nullified by the power of the cross. Galatians 3:13 says, *"Christ redeemed us from the curse of the law by becoming a curse for us."* I proclaim my freedom from every generational curse, every spoken curse, and every witchcraft attack. I am washed clean by the blood of Jesus.

I declare that I walk in the light of God's truth, and the lies of darkness have no power over me. Psalm 27:1 affirms, *"The Lord is my light and my salvation; whom shall I fear?"* I reject every lie, deception, and manipulation of the enemy. I stand on the truth of God's Word and declare victory over the powers of darkness.

I stand firm in these declarations, knowing that God's Word is powerful and cannot be broken, and that God is faithful to bring deliverance and victory in every area of my life. I trust in His promises and rest in His unfailing love.

Prayer of Deliverance

1. Heavenly Father, I declare that I break free from the cycle of fear of failure. Your perfect love casts out all fear. (1 John 4:18)
2. Lord, I renounce every spirit of fear that has held me back from stepping into new opportunities. I embrace courage and confidence in your power, in the name of Jesus Christ. (2 Timothy 1:7)
3. I declare that I am more than a conqueror through Christ Jesus who strengthens me. Failure has no power over me. (Romans 8:37)
4. Father, I release all past failures into your hands. I am a new creation in Christ, and I trust in your redemption and restoration. (2 Corinthians 5:17)
5. I decree and declare that I have the mind of Christ, and I am filled with wisdom and understanding to seize new opportunities with confidence. (1 Corinthians 2:16)
6. Lord, I reject the lies of the enemy that try to convince me of my inadequacy. Your grace is sufficient for me, and your power is made perfect in my weakness. (2 Corinthians 12:9)
7. I break every generational curse of fear of failure in my family line. I declare freedom and breakthrough in the name of Jesus. (Galatians 3:13-14)

8. Heavenly Father, I surrender my fears and anxieties to you. I cast all my cares upon you, knowing that you care for me. (1 Peter 5:7)
9. I declare that the Lord goes before me, and He makes a way where there seems to be no way. I step out in faith, trusting in His guidance and provision, in the name of Jesus Christ. (Isaiah 43:19)
10. Lord, I receive a spirit of boldness and courage. I am not ashamed or afraid to pursue new opportunities, for you are with me wherever I go. (Joshua 1:9)
11. I declare that I am equipped with the full armor of God, including the shield of faith, which extinguishes all the fiery darts of fear, in the name of Jesus Christ. (Ephesians 6:16)
12. Heavenly Father, I rebuke the spirit of fear and timidity. I receive a spirit of power, love, and a sound mind to face every new opportunity with confidence. (2 Timothy 1:7)
13. I declare that I am rooted and established in the love of Christ. I am filled with His perfect love, which casts out all fear. (Ephesians 3:17-19)
14. Lord, I break every stronghold of fear that has hindered my progress and success. I am released to step into new opportunities fearlessly, in the name of Jesus Christ. (2 Corinthians 10:4)
15. I declare that failure is not my identity. I am a child of God, redeemed by the blood of Jesus, and destined for greatness. (1 Peter 2:9)
16. I renounce the spirit of perfectionism and embrace a spirit of excellence. I do all things as unto the Lord, knowing that His grace is sufficient for me. (Colossians 3:23-24)
17. Lord, I choose faith over fear. I trust in your promises and believe that you will lead me into victory and success, in the name of Jesus Christ. (Hebrews 11:6)

18. I declare that I have been given a spirit of adoption as a child of God. I am accepted, loved, and chosen by Him, regardless of any past failures. (Romans 8:15-16)
19. Heavenly Father, I release forgiveness to myself for any past mistakes or failures. I receive your mercy and grace to move forward with confidence. (Ephesians 1:7)
20. I declare that the Holy Spirit empowers me to overcome every fear and step into new opportunities with courage and boldness, in the name of Jesus Christ. (Acts 1:8)
21. Lord, I break the power of negative thoughts and self-doubt, in the name of Jesus Christ. I choose to meditate on your truth and embrace a mindset of victory and success. (Philippians 4:8)
22. I declare that God's plans for me are plans for good and not for harm, to give me a future and a hope. I trust in His faithfulness and guidance. (Jeremiah 29:11)
23. I renounce the fear of rejection. I am accepted and approved by God, and I boldly pursue new opportunities with confidence in His love for me. (Romans 8:31)
24. I declare that God is my refuge and strength, a very present help in times of trouble. I find courage and confidence in His presence. (Psalm 46:1-2)
25. Lord, I rebuke the spirit of procrastination and complacency. I embrace a spirit of diligence and perseverance, seizing new opportunities with enthusiasm. (Proverbs 13:4)
26. I declare that I am an overcomer by the blood of the Lamb and the word of my testimony. Failure has no power over me. (Revelation 12:11)
27. I renounce the spirit of comparison and competition. I am fearfully and wonderfully made, uniquely gifted to fulfill my purpose with confidence. (Psalm 139:14)
28. I declare that the favor of God surrounds me like a shield. I step into new opportunities, knowing that His favor goes before me. (Psalm 5:12)

29. Lord, I break every bondage of fear that has kept me confined. I embrace the freedom and liberty to explore new horizons and embrace new challenges. (Galatians 5:1)
30. I declare that my steps are ordered by the Lord. He directs my path and leads me into the opportunities He has prepared for me. (Proverbs 3:5-6)
31. Heavenly Father, I release any feelings of inadequacy and embrace the truth that your strength is made perfect in my weakness, in the name of Jesus Christ. (2 Corinthians 12:9)
32. I declare that I have been given a spirit of power, love, and a sound mind. Fear of failure has no place in my life, in the name of Jesus Christ. (2 Timothy 1:7)
33. Lord, I break the cycle of fear that has held me back. I choose to step out in faith, trusting that You will make a way for me. (Isaiah 41:10)
34. I declare that I can do all things through Christ who strengthens me. Failure is not an option when I rely on His power. (Philippians 4:13)
35. I renounce the spirit of timidity and embrace a spirit of boldness. I am filled with the Holy Spirit, who empowers me to overcome every fear. (Acts 4:31)
36. I declare that I am anointed by God to succeed. I am equipped with everything I need to excel in every new opportunity. (1 John 2:20)
37. Lord, I surrender my fear of failure to you. I trust in your sovereignty and believe that you work all things together for my good. (Romans 8:28)
38. I renounce the spirit of fear and embrace a spirit of faith. I step into new opportunities, knowing that with God, all things are possible. (Mark 9:23)
39. I declare that I am a vessel of honor, set apart for God's purposes. I break free from the fear of failure and embrace my divine calling. (2 Timothy 2:21)

40. Lord, I reject the lies of the enemy that try to discourage me. I choose to meditate on your promises, which fill me with courage and confidence. (Psalm 119:148)
41. I declare that I am not defined by my past failures. I am a new creation in Christ, and I walk in His victory and redemption. (2 Corinthians 5:17)
42. Heavenly Father, I break every agreement I have made with fear and failure. I align my thoughts and declarations with your truth and promises. (Romans 12:2)
43. I renounce the spirit of fear that paralyzes me. I embrace a spirit of action and step into new opportunities with boldness and assurance. (James 2:17)
44. I declare that I am rooted in God's love, and His love drives out all fear. I walk in the confidence of His unfailing love for me. (1 John 4:16-18)
45. Lord, I release any negative words spoken over me that have contributed to my fear of failure, in the name of Jesus Christ. I receive your words of life and speak them over myself. (Proverbs 18:21)
46. I declare that failure is not the end but an opportunity for growth and learning. I embrace the lessons and rise above my past mistakes. (Philippians 3:13-14)
47. I renounce the spirit of timidity and embrace a spirit of power. I am bold and courageous, stepping into new opportunities with faith and confidence. (Romans 1:16)
48. I declare that I am fearfully and wonderfully made, created for greatness. I reject the fear of failure and walk in the assurance of my identity in Christ. (Psalm 139:14)
49. Lord, I surrender my need for control and perfection. I trust in your perfect plan for my life and step into new opportunities with surrendered faith. (Proverbs 16:9)

50. I declare that God's grace is sufficient for me. In His strength, I overcome fear of failure and step into new opportunities with boldness and assurance. (2 Corinthians 12:9)

Made in the USA
Coppell, TX
16 March 2025